Eliot,

Hope you enjoy this trip
down memory lane.
Some good memories, some not...
but all are funny ☺

Appreciate you,
      Matt T

.s I dont know if this makes sense
    but...

    .. youre my hallelujah

Management Is Dead:
The 5 Keys to Unlock Employee Retention, Skyrocket ROI, and Lead a Revolution

© 2023 by Leadr, Inc.

Published by Leadr Inc., 5360 Legacy Dr suite 180, Plano, TX 75024.

The stories in this book are based on both authors' recollections of events. Some names and characters have been changed, some events compressed or combined, and some dialogue altered or recreated for clarity and/or to protect identities.

Cataloging-in-Publication Data is available from the Library of Congress.
ISBN 979-8-9880553-0-3 (print) | ISBN 979-8-9880553-1-0 (paperback) | ISBN 979-8-9880553-2-7 (ebook)

MANAGEMENT IS

DEAD

THE 5 KEYS TO UNLOCK EMPLOYEE RETENTION, SKYROCKET ROI, AND LEAD A REVOLUTION

BY MATT TRESIDDER & CHRIS HEASLIP

Note: The stories in this book are based on both authors' recollections of events. Some names and characteristics have been changed, some events compressed or combined, and some dialogue altered or recreated for clarity and to protect identities.

DEDICATIONS

To my wife, Sarah, and our three children.
Without your love and support over the years,
the words in this book would not be possible.

And to my mom:
Thank you for your hard work and sacrifice
that helped us get where we are today.
We wouldn't be here without you.

-CHRIS

They say leadership is lonely - but it doesn't have to be.
This book is dedicated to my wife, Kiasa.
Without her, none of this is possible.

To the entire Leadr team:
Here's to developing 1 million leaders & beyond.

-MATT

CONTENTS

Introduction: Management Is Dead   8

Part 1: Redefining the Landscape

Ch. 1 Why Leadership Matters   23

Ch. 2 People Development   44

Part 2: The Five Foundations of People Development

Ch. 3 Recognizing Unique Strengths   59

Ch. 4 Personalized Growth Plans   73

Ch. 5 Setting Clear Goals   88

Ch. 6 1-on-1 Meetings   110

Ch. 7 Giving Effective Feedback   133

Epilogue: Going Forward   156

Acknowledgments   163

Appendix A   166

Appendix B   169

Appendix C   173

INTRODUCTION

MANAGEMENT
IS DEAD

CHRIS

Let's talk about Bob. My gut says you've encountered your own "Bob." And Bob is a big reason why this book exists.

Bob came to us as a seasoned and proven sales manager. He had years of experience in the church software space. He was perfect for what we were doing at Pushpay, the software company I co-founded in 2011.

The goal was simple: Make the monetary, non-profit donation process as easy as buying a song on iTunes. "Just push pay" was our mantra. We had been hitting our targets, but we wanted to turbo the business. We were eyeing 900 customers for our next quarter, and we needed to ensure we hit that ambitious goal.

Enter Bob.

Bob not only delivered on our goal, he exceeded it. We didn't just secure 900 customers that quarter; we hit 996. We were happy, the employees were satisfied, and the investors were ecstatic. We felt on top of the world. What could possibly go wrong?

Everything.

Bob was a southern gentleman through and through, complete with a disarming twang. On his first day at the office, he walked in with a blue, collared shirt tucked into his pleated khaki pants with shiny brown dress shoes and a leather belt to match. His receding hairline was slicked to the side and, from the moment he walked into the office, his bombastic southern greeting to our receptionist echoed through the office.

However, the sales team mostly consisted of two kinds of millennials. There were the ones with skinny jeans and t-shirts long enough to be skirts, and another group that mirrored the skinny jeans but traded in their t-shirts for an array of flannels that resembled lumberjack uniforms. Both types were obsessed with coffee. Many even had their favorite kombuchas or IPA beers. They were a vivid example of the changing workforce.

And they couldn't be more different than Bob.

Whereas the sales team was nimble and free-flowing, Bob was not. His management style was "my way or the highway." For starters, he had very structured sales scripts. Everything on a call was planned to a T. Deviate and die. At times you could actually walk past sales reps and hear them talking in unison to different people on the phone, mimicking one another right down to the inflection points in their voices, which Bob would have them practice. He once corrected a rep for saying "you all" instead of "y'all" to a customer from the South.

For a while, it worked, hence us not just meeting but exceeding our quarterly sales goal. But after just a few short months, the novelty wore off. Sales numbers began plateauing, with no outlook for recovery. Then they plummeted - and plummeted hard.

The team was retreating, growing increasingly frustrated with the lack of freedom to do what they did best: read their customers, adjust, and tailor their approach. And while Bob would put in the extra hours to try and work with the team, we eventually hit the point of diminishing returns. After three months of declining sales, I knew something had to change.

In January 2016, I called a meeting with Bob, our VP of marketing, and our sales director, Matt Tresidder.

MATT

Hey, I'm the Matt he's talking about and the co-author of this book.

CHRIS

Our VP of marketing and Bob laid out their plan for turning things around. To my chagrin, Bob wanted to double down on what was not working. Sure, he said he'd tweak his scripts, but, in the end, it was all about his rigid process. There was no mention of genuinely getting to know and understand his team, how each person worked best and responded to his leadership, and how focusing on an individual's strengths might help fix our dilemma. He was a robot – albeit a kind, nicely-dressed one – that wanted to lead robots.

After Bob walked out, I asked Matt to stay behind. I had an idea—a thought experiment of sorts. I asked Matt to send me a proposal of what he would do if he were in Bob's shoes. I wanted fresh blood, I wanted a new way forward, and I wanted a clean start.

Matt agreed and said he would work on something over the weekend. In other words, I was giving Matt an audition, although he had no clue.

MATT

I really had no clue. I thought I was just doing Chris a favor.

CHRIS

At this critical juncture, I felt the weight of being the CEO. The Sunday of that important weekend wasn't any better. The knot in my stomach tightened as Monday neared the horizon. Matt didn't make it any easier when he sent his proposal for the sales team late Sunday night, ahead of when I had asked for it.

And it was incredible.

The plan was a detailed, 10-page document outlining the perfect solution to our problem. It spelled out what each sales team member would be responsible for, who should be hired and fired, and where we should move people to set them up for success. It described how Matt would get rid of the bottom performers and give those opportunities to the high performers, thus weeding out the anchors and giving the rock stars more autonomy. All of this, he explained, would both raise our numbers and rebuild the dismal morale that had plagued the sales floor after months of missed targets, robotic sales calls, and top-down management.

But the most important thing Matt's plan laid out was how he would get to know the team. Really get to know them. He would understand not only where they wanted to go in our company but also in life. He would treat them like human beings, not like robots. He would collaborate with them, not simply manage them.

That spoke to me, and my excitement skyrocketed.

After receiving the proposal, I asked Matt if he would be willing to step into

Bob's role on an interim basis if we made a change. He was surprised but said yes. It was now clear what I had to do.

When I approached Bob about the change, he led with excuses. He blamed the weather, the timing, the season. Everything. I debunked every one of them, and, little by little, we came to an understanding that he wasn't the right guy. Sure, he had the team's ear, but he didn't have their heart. And that was a problem.

After nearly an hour, I stood up, shook Bob's hand, and gave him one last goodbye. HR escorted him out of his office and gave him the quintessential small box to collect his belongings. It was one of the hardest and best decisions I ever made. The era of robotic scripts was over. The era of tight, buttoned-up, top-down leadership was over. The era of imposing our stiff demands was over. At that moment, people management was over, and people development was born.

It changed the course of the business, and it changed the course of my life. And it's why we're here, writing this to you today.

MATT

Before we go any further, let me make something clear. I don't pretend to have some sort of magic business touch. I don't have a crystal ball. And I didn't go about making drastic, across-the-board changes.

I didn't change our value proposition.

I didn't change the product.

I fired a few poor fits, but 90% of the people didn't change.

So what changed after I took over? The biggest thing I did was invest in our people. I talked with them. I met with them. That made people feel like they had a voice for the first time in years. They felt seen and heard.

See, one of the biggest contributing factors to team health, and ultimately success and retention, is the relationship people have with their manager. And yet too many leaders take that for granted. Frankly, they're terrible at it. They do it half-heartedly, or just to "check a box," or they do it because HR tells them they have to.

There's no attention, and there's certainly no collaboration.

And that leads us to where we are today at Leadr. To a new way forward.

CHRIS AND MATT

Out of all the things we could kick off a book with, why did we start with the story of Bob? Because we have a secret to share with you: How you're running your company and managing your employees is all wrong. In fact, it's killing your organization and you are paying the price.

How do we know? Because we've done it the wrong way, the old way. Together, we built Pushpay into a billion-dollar company and revolutionized how people made donations online. That led to a revolution in the giving space. We loved it, our customers loved it, and our investors loved it. But during the process of building that company – and reflecting on it after – we discovered something about how we ran things that changed the course of our lives. It wasn't about balance sheets, investments, or even going public. It was about the relationship between managers and employees.

In short, we learned that, for too long, we had led our people the wrong way. When we shifted away from Bob, when we learned from Bob's mistakes and our own, that's when the company truly took off.

That led us to realize a better way. A new way. A more complete way. A way that is the future. And we'd like to share it with you so you aren't left behind. It's the key to freeing yourself up, retaining your best people, and increasing your return on investment (ROI).

This new way is called people development. That's opposed to people management, which is what nearly everyone is doing now. That's what Bob did. But that leads to resignations, burnout, and wasted time, money, and resources.

Put bluntly, management is dead. The type of management that's all about taking charge of something, handling, directing, controlling, and ordering, has given way to developing, which focuses on bringing out the possibilities in people and helping them grow and expand. You manage your finances. You develop relationships.

Ask yourself this, then: Would you rather be managed or developed?

We think the answer is clear. But don't take our word for it. According to Gallup's State of the Global Workplace, just 33% of workers feel they are thriving, and a paltry 21% of employees are actually engaged at work[1]. Employee stress? That's at an all-time high.

That's the world of people management.

We don't have to tell you that those numbers are awful. But we do have to tell you what those numbers mean for your business: employee turnover, lost ROI, and customer churn, just to name a few. If you can't attract and retain top

---

1 "State of the Global Workplace Report." Gallup, 2022, https://www.gallup.com/workplace/349484/state-of-the-global-workplace.aspx

talent, your business isn't going to survive.

But the point of this book isn't just to tell you the problems with people management. The point is to show you the better way, the future.

That future is people development.

People development is an important shift in how you approach your employees. In the old way — people management — employers treat employees as commodities to be harvested. Bosses squeeze every last ounce of productivity out of their salespeople, for instance, and use carrots and plenty of sticks to motivate and get what they want. It's a world of tight dress codes and even tighter sales scripts. When that gets old (and it gets old quickly), those employees burn out, become dissatisfied, or trade you in for a new gig. And the cycle starts over again. Rinse and repeat, rinse and repeat.

That cycle creates too many headaches, too much lost revenue, and too much wasted energy. You can't move your business forward if you're constantly replacing your employees, which is massively expensive.

In fact, another Gallup statistic estimates that "the cost of replacing an individual employee can range from one-half to two times the employee's annual salary — and that's a conservative estimate."[2]

So what does that look like practically? "A 100-person organization that provides an average salary of $50,000 could have turnover and replacement costs of approximately $660,000 to $2.6 million per year." We aren't talking about big corporations here. We're talking about small to medium businesses, like yours, which are the backbone of our economy. And yet those costs don't

---

2 "This Fixable Problem Costs U.S. Businesses $1 Trillion." Gallup, March 2019, https://www.gallup.com/workplace/247391/fixable-problem-costs-businesses-trillion.aspx

even begin to factor in the lost institutional knowledge.

Here's the kicker: "Fifty-two percent of voluntarily exiting employees say their manager or organization could have done something to prevent them from leaving their job."

In short, you're losing people, losing money, and losing company knowledge because of people management. You're empowering the "Bobs" of the world, giving them free rein to tank your company. And a massive chunk of all of that is preventable.

Yet the problem is still growing. According to one study by Future Forum, 63% of Americans are open to looking for a new job in the next year.[3]

And before you think this can all be explained away by, "The new workforce is just entitled and wants more money," consider a 2020 Work Institute report. This report exposed that the number one reason people left their jobs voluntarily is because of "career development." The least important reason? "Compensation and benefits."[4] In other words, people are leaving not because they want you to pay them more but because they want you to develop them more.

That's why people development is so important.

In the people development way, there's an understanding – an agreement – made between employer and employee. In that way, the employer asks the employee what they want for themselves and where they want to go and then shows them how to get there.

---

3 "The Great Executive-Employee Disconnect." Slack, October 2021. https://futureforum.com/wp-content/up-loads/2021/10/Future-Forum-Pulse-Report-October-2021.pdf

4 "2020 Retention Report." Work Institute, 2020, https://info.workinstitute.com/hubfs/2020%20Retention%20Report/Work%20Institutes%202020%20Retention%20Report.pdf

In a word, it's collaborative. It's what Matt did when he took over for Bob.

That's because employees today want to have a say, a voice. They want to be engaged by their bosses. And most importantly, they want to be invested in. We created a simple graphic to show you the difference between the old and new ways and where your focus should be. In short, you need to start with a mission, then build the team with the right people, and then you'll see the results.

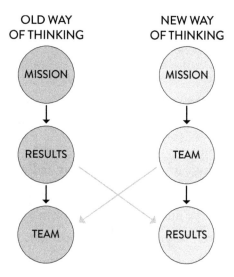

There's an old saying that if you give a man a fish, you feed him for a day but teach a man to fish and you feed him for a lifetime. Here's the employee development version: Tell an employee what to do, and you get their time; dialogue with an employee about what they want and where they want to go, and you get their passion.

Bob never had our employees' passion.

Here's the reality: This isn't your grandparents' workplace anymore. It isn't even your father's or your mother's workplace anymore.

In the past, workplaces were autocratic fiefdoms where Bob's top-down leadership reigned. The boss made the decisions and the rules, based many times on personal preferences, and workers were expected to be aligned, alienated, or axed.

That's not how the next generations in the workforce are wired. And by "generations" we're not just talking about Millennials. Some Millennials are now in their 40s! In other words, this isn't about catering to a small percentage of younger employees. It's about understanding what motivates this new era's workforce. To get this new workforce to even show up for work (i.e., the most basic of tasks), you have to have their buy-in. Said simply, you have to collaborate with them.

So what do you do? You can go three routes:

1. You can ignore the changing landscape and double down on autocratic leadership. But in the end, you and your business will fail because that's not how this workforce responds.

2. You can take the Google approach. You can hire top talent, tell them how special they are at every turn, and pamper them with so many extras that they don't want to – and can't – leave. But there are maybe three companies that can afford that: Disney, Meta, and Google. You are not one of them. Plus, the incredible pressure and expectations that employees face as a result of those benefits will still lead to burnout.

3. You can take the new approach, where you make a deal with your employees and develop them[5]. They give you their time and attention, and you invest in them. Managers and employees come together in a loosely-made bargain: The company gets the work, and the employees get to be heard, learn, and grow. It's a collaboration that finds the overlap between the goals of the company and the employee. Everyone wins.

---

5 We created an entire company on this new approach called Leadr. More on that in a minute.

Not surprisingly, we think the third way is best, not only because it considers the DNA of the new workforce, but because it's also the most rewarding and sustainable – both for you and your business.

We learned this the hard way with Bob. And we came to understand what Gallup sums up in the Global Workplace 2022 Report:

The real fix is this simple: better leaders in the workplace. Managers need to be better listeners, coaches, and collaborators. Great managers help colleagues learn and grow, recognize their colleagues for doing great work, and make them truly feel cared about. In environments like this, workers thrive.

That's why we founded a new company, Leadr, which is all about people development. Our goal? Develop 1 million leaders in this new workforce. We hired the best talent, built a platform from the ground up to deliver that training, and now we want to unveil the building blocks of that idea – and how to implement it – to you. It's what we're passionate about. It's not only the future, but it's here. Now. And it's why management is dead.

BOOK STRUCTURE

We co-wrote this book for a very specific reason. Both of us have our own stories and experiences that contribute to giving you a complete picture of where we've been and where we're headed. We'll note who is talking (or writing, in this case) when necessary. You've seen that already.

This book is also based on what we call "The 5 Foundations." These foundations are the building blocks of people development. They are:

- Recognizing Unique Strengths
- Personalized Growth Plans

- Setting Clear Goals
- 1-on-1 Meetings
- Giving Effective Feedback

We'll dedicate a chapter to each of these, unpacking the right and wrong ways to approach them, explaining how embracing each concept affects your bottom line, and highlighting the key concepts with personal stories. We've also included practical tools in the appendix you can use to start implementing everything you've learned right now.

After reading this book, we believe you'll transform yourself and your company. You'll become a part of the new wave of leadership that, quite frankly, you can't afford to ignore.

People development is the new way forward. It's not a fad; it's a foundation. Ignore it, and you'll be left behind. Embrace it, and you'll be a part of the revolution. Implement it, and you'll reap incredible benefits.

Let's move forward. Together.

PART 1

REDEFINING THE LANDSCAPE

CHAPTER 1

WHY LEADERSHIP MATTERS

MATT

I'll never forget the day I was ambushed.

In 2016 I was serving as the VP of sales at Pushpay. I had been in that role for about six months after the Bob fiasco. I was confident that I was getting the hang of things, and our numbers reflected that.

That all came to a screeching halt one summer afternoon.

It was late in the day, about 3 o'clock, on a Wednesday. I got a coded instant message from one of our top sales performers, Jake.

"Hey Matt, are you free to catch up?" he asked.

It certainly wasn't odd for Jake to want to chat. After all, I had intentionally opened up the lines of communication between managers and employees in the last six months. But this just felt different. It was abrupt, and, on top of that, I had already interacted with Jake earlier in the day.

I told him, "Sure," but since it lacked details, I included a question mark at the end to hint at my slight confusion.

"Great. I'm in the conference room at the back. Can you come join us?" Jake responded.

"Us?" I asked.

"Yeah, it's not just me."

I went from slightly confused to worried. What is this all about?

Regardless, I got up from my desk and made my way to the conference room at the absolute back of the office building, secluded from prying eyes and curious ears, which also told me something bigger was brewing.

After making the long trek, I opened the conference room door and was shocked at what I saw. In front of me was the entire team huddled around the table, with a seat reserved for me at the front. They all looked up with shy, slightly guilty expressions.

I slowly walked in and sat down. My mind was racing about what was about to happen.

"Heeeeey, guys," I said slowly. "What's going on?"

The entire team started shifting nervously in their seats. No one immediately spoke up, as if they were telepathically drawing straws to see who would break the silence and the news.

"Jake, just tell me what's going on," I said, this time a little more forcefully.

"Matt," he began, taking a deep breath and getting straight to the point. "Things have gotten so bad with Nigel. We absolutely can't stand it anymore. And if you don't fire him, we're all handing in our resignations today and walking."

My stomach knotted up. My heart began beating faster. I felt like the rapper, Eminem, "palms sweaty, knees weak, arms are heavy."[7] Nigel was the team's direct manager and was nowhere to be seen. In other words, it became clear that this was a full-blown mutiny, and I was right in the middle.

I had a decision to make. Do I get upset? Do I throw my arms up? Do I scold them and walk out?

Absolutely not. I recognized the gravity of the moment and wanted to use it as an opportunity to unite the team and prove that, even though this may not be the best way to do it, we can have hard conversations and that people with concerns will be heard.

That said, I knew I couldn't just fire Nigel over concerns I had never heard before, but I also knew I couldn't afford to lose an entire sales division. And I could tell the team was serious. While being threatened with a mass exodus is never fun, I knew I needed to listen to them. Truly listen.

So that's what I did. I gave a long, drawn-out "OK" and then told them to explain what was happening. I gripped the arms of my chair and listened as their concerns shot out like a fire hose on full blast. Here's what they said:

They were burned out and beaten down by Nigel's management style.
He was giving them conflicting directions.
He was a micromanager at times.
He was too hands-off at others.

---

7 Eminem, "Lose Yourself." Genius. https://genius.com/Eminem-lose-yourself-lyrics

He didn't coach them.

He was proscriptive.

He would regularly miss 1-on-1 meetings with team members.

He wasn't listening.

He didn't care.

It went on and on.

All of that was hard to hear for two reasons. First, Nigel wasn't a bad person. I knew him well. Second, in some ways, this entire ordeal reflected on me as well. I realized I wasn't as plugged into the pulse of those under me as I thought I was.

So I sat silently and took notes. Ultimately, it became clear the team in front of me was craving development, and Nigel lacked the ability to see nuance and understand how to relate to his team as individuals. He was either the absentee manager who was never around or the micromanager who refused to extend trust or autonomy to the team.

A picture started to emerge: If this team was ever going to become a high-performing team – which should be the goal of every manager and team in a company – it probably wasn't going to happen with Nigel at the helm. These were some of the most talented people we had in the company. Historically, they had crushed their goals. But their leader wasn't leading them. He had the potential to be leading a team of Picassos, but instead, he had them drawing stick figures.

Still, that didn't mean I could fire Nigel on the spot. If I valued developing people, I also had to extend that courtesy to him. And so, I sent Nigel a similar message to the one Jake sent me and asked him to join us in the back conference room. When he walked in, he had what I could only assume was the same look on his face that I had on mine when I opened the door an hour earlier.

As he sat down, I began explaining the team's concerns. I tried to make it obvious to both him and them that I wasn't taking sides, but rather working as an intermediary. As I listed off their concerns, with input from Jake, Nigel broke down. In fact, he started bawling.

"I know I haven't been doing a good job," he said through sobs. "I feel like I've been sucking at work as a boss and at home as a father. I know I can do better. I swear I'm trying my very best. I'm just stressed and overwhelmed. I wanna do better. I can do better."

The mood of the room instantly changed. The team felt heard, and they saw Nigel as a human being. Both sides agreed to give each other a do-over.

So what happened from there?

Eventually, we had to move Nigel to a different role on a different team, which was a win for everyone.

Why? Because even though Nigel recognized his weaknesses, and even though the team backed off their mutiny and gave him another chance, in the following weeks, it became clear that Nigel didn't have the ability to lead a high-performing team.

And that's the point of this entire story. Leadership matters. You can't have a non-high performer leading a team of high performers.[8] And that brings us to the law of the lid.

---

8 We'll cover an important caveat on this later. Stay tuned, as they say.

CHRIS AND MATT

LAW OF THE LID

We've become obsessed with "The Law of the Lid." It's foundational to who we are and what we've built at Leadr. The phrase and concept come from business and leadership guru John Maxwell.

The idea is that your leadership abilities (or lack thereof) drastically affect your team's (and your company's) success in more ways than you think. At first glance, that may seem obvious. And, on the one hand, it is a simple concept. But it's one of those simple concepts with deep roots and deeper implications. It's an onion with layers to be peeled back.

Here's how Maxwell himself puts it:

> Leadership ability is the lid that determines a person's level of effectiveness. The lower an individual's ability to lead, the lower the lid on his potential. The higher the individual's ability to lead, the higher the lid on his potential. To give you an example, if your leadership rates an 8, then your effectiveness can never be greater than a 7. If your leadership is only a 4, then your effectiveness will be no higher than a 3. Your leadership ability—for better or for worse—always determines your effectiveness and the potential impact of your organization.[9]

See what we mean? But here's where we'll take it a step further. While Maxwell focuses more on your personal implications, we focus heavily on the implications for the company. In our experience, it isn't just about your personal potential, but the company's potential. It isn't just about where you can go, but where

---

9 John Maxwell, "The Law of the Lid,"John Maxwell, July 2019, https://www.johnmaxwell.com/blog/the-law-of-the-lid/

your team can go and where your organization can go.

Before we go any further, you may be tempted to compare The Law of the Lid to the old adage, "Never ask someone to do something you're not willing to do yourself." The idea is that if you're not willing to dig a ditch, don't ask your employee to do it. But this is different. It's bigger. It's not about what you're willing to do; it's about your leadership and how it builds up or tears down those around you. You can't expect your team to perform at a high level if you can't lead them well. That's bigger and has many more far-reaching implications. Maxwell touches on this briefly when he sums it up: "Without leadership ability, a person's impact is only a fraction of what it could be with good leadership. Whatever you will accomplish is restricted by your ability to lead others."

That key word is "impact." The Law of the Lid is about your impact. Not just on your future, but on the future of those around you and the company you're a part of.

Whether you realize it or not, you've seen this play out. How many times in your own professional life have you seen the lackadaisical approach of a team leader bring down the effectiveness of the entire team? Or how many times have you seen a manager intentionally stifle a high performer because they're worried that the high performer will outshine them and "make them look bad"?

Are we hitting a nerve?

Consider this from a CNBC article:

> Millennial workers feel [disgruntled] most acutely when they don't have
> strong, inspiring leadership at their companies, for example: Of those who
> say they're not proud of the place they work, 70 percent of them say that's
> the top reason why.[10]

And remember, Millennials are now the dominant group in the workforce.

That's where Nigel comes in. Everyone has a Nigel story. We do. You do. Your
relatives do. How do we know? Because failed leadership is an epidemic in
businesses. It always has been. And it's a huge factor in "The Great Resignation."

THE GREAT RESIGNATION

What are four of the worst words you can hear as a manager? I'll tell you my
four, and I think you'll agree: "Hey, can we talk?"

When you hear or see those words, you get that sinking feeling in your stomach.
Your heart races a bit. Maybe you even start sweating. Why? Because you know
exactly what's coming. A resignation. A lost employee. Institutional knowledge
and talent that walks out the door.

Welcome to The Great Resignation.

In the wake of the coronavirus pandemic, workers quit their jobs at record
levels.[11] Not just close to record levels, but actual record numbers. We had

---

10 Zameena Mjia, "Nearly 9 out of 10 Millennials Would Consider Taking a Pay Cut to Get This." CNBC, June 2018.
https://www.cnbc.com/2018/06/27/nearly-9-out-of-10-millennials-would-consider-a-pay-cut-to-get-this.html

11 Eli Rosenberg, "4.3 Million Americans Left Their jobs in December as Omicron Variant Disrupted Everything." The
Washington Post, February 2022. https://www.washingtonpost.com/business/2022/02/01/job-quits-resignations-
december-2021/

never seen this many people voluntarily quit their jobs and move on to something else.

Why? As we said in the introduction, this isn't just about pay. It's not that people woke up after quarantine and suddenly wanted more money. Employees have wanted more money since people first started trading work for wealth.

That's a constant. So what happened? During quarantine, people realigned their priorities. They realized they want – they need – to work for people who value them. People who want to develop them. People who will listen. They want to believe in you and your company. No matter what you think, money can't cover a multitude of sins, especially management sins. And the workplace is filled with bad managers committing too many management sins.

"A new Pew Research Center survey finds that low pay, a lack of opportunities for advancement, and feeling disrespected at work are the top reasons why Americans quit their jobs last year," Pew Research wrote in March 2022.[12] And while pay is mentioned, you can't ignore the other two reasons: "lack of opportunities for advancement" and "feeling disrespected at work."

In fact, that Pew survey found that pay and "lack of opportunities for advancement" were tied as the top reasons cited by people for leaving their jobs (63%). And "feeling disrespected" was cited a whopping 57% of the time, only six percentage points behind the top spot.

It all supports exactly what Maxwell lays out in the Law of the Lid—your leadership ability matters. And if your leadership is lacking, you'll never have a

---

12 Kim Parker and Juliana Menasce Horowitz, "Majority of Workers Who Quit a Job in 2021 Cite Low Pya, No Opportunties for Advancement, Feeling Disrespected." Pew Research Center, March 2022. https://www.pewresearch.org/fact-tank/2022/03/09/majority-of-workers-who-quit-a-job-in-2021-cite-low-pay-no-opportunities-for-advancement-feeling-disrespected/

13 Annie Duke, "Why Quitting is Underrated." The Atlantic, September 2022. https://www.theatlantic.com/ideas/archive/2022/09/why-quitting-is-underrated/671562/

high-performing team. And you're going to continue bleeding people.

It's exactly why we've recently seen another phenomenon storm onto the scene: quiet quitting. This term perfectly sums up what happens when you fail to lead, when you can't lead, because you yourself are not growing.

What exactly is "quiet quitting"? The Atlantic describes it as "staying in a job [you] no longer like while doing the minimum necessary to hold on to it."[13]

In other words, it's when people have lost their passion and aren't willing to go above and beyond. Instead, they slink along, doing the bare minimum. And in a post-pandemic world with this new workforce, you better believe it's on the rise.

Just look at the data from Google trends on the topic:

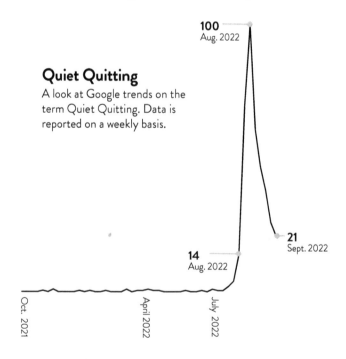

100
Aug. 2022

Quiet Quitting
A look at Google trends on the term Quiet Quitting. Data is reported on a weekly basis.

21
Sept. 2022

14
Aug. 2022

Oct. 2021

April 2022

July 2022

Let's be clear: Quiet quitting isn't new. The term may be, but the concept has been around for years. In fact, quiet quitting is exactly why we do what we do at Leadr. It all comes down to one thing: managers being disconnected from their employees. In other words, people are quiet quitting at record numbers because they're not engaged, they're not developed, they're not seen, and they're not heard.

We saw at Pushpay what the labor market is seeing now – people quitting in their heads but staying physically after they've decided to leave mentally. I've heard one person put it like this: "Don't worry about the people leaving your team; worry about the people that are still there but have already left in their heads." They're willing to check all the basic boxes while looking for the next thing. They're just waiting for the perfect opportunity, and you're paying them to find it.

If you don't know or can't see that, then you're not connected to your people. How do you stop people from quiet quitting, then? How do you actually make sure they're high performers and you're leading a high-performing team? It comes down to collaboration.

You can't dictate to this workforce. You have to develop this workforce. You have to create an environment where their work has a deep meaning attached to it – both for them and the company. Now, more than ever, if you can't articulate why the work they're doing matters, they're going to check out.

You have to show them that what they're working towards and why they're working towards it matters.

CHRIS

THE IMPORTANCE OF MISSION

I think it's important to dig into the idea of meaningful work because it's absolutely essential. After starting 17 companies, I can tell you employees want to know that they're growing, but they also want to know they're having an impact. They want to believe in what they're doing. But unfortunately, too many companies today don't have a compelling mission. Sure, they have a mission statement, but they don't have an actual mission – something their employees can truly rally around.

That's why I hate mission statements. Too many times, mission statements let companies off the hook. That's because a lot of companies think they can have a brainstorm, employ 25 people to come up with a few sentences (that get watered down because of decision-by-committee), put out a mission statement, and then they're good. But rarely do mission statements have an ethos, a soul. Instead, they allow a company to check the box of "we created a mission statement" and then move on without embodying it.

There's an absolutely insane statistic on this subject that shows just how much you need to embrace a mission and not just a mission statement. According to LinkedIn, a massive 71% of professionals say they would "be willing to take a pay cut to work for a company that has a mission they believe in and shared values."[14]

I know we keep hammering this point, but employees aren't just concerned about the money. That's the old way of thinking. And it's an irresponsible way of thinking. If you think money is going to fix all your problems – if you think throwing raises at your disgruntled employees will make them stay –

---

14 Nina McQueen, "Workplace Culture Trends: The Key to Hiring (and Keeping) Top Talent in 2018." LinkedIn, June 2018, https://blog.linkedin.com/2018/june/26/workplace-culture-trends-the-key-to-hiring-and-keeping-top-talent

then you're going to keep losing people, and you're going to run out of money. You have to give them a compelling mission. It's just that simple.

"While earning potential is always going to be an important aspect of a job, the company's culture is what motivates and inspires workers on a daily basis," Nina McQueen, LinkedIn vice president of benefits and experience, says.[15]

Recently, at one of our Leadr all-hands meetings – where the entire company gathers to consistently get alignment on our mission – we experienced a vivid example of this. In those meetings, we regularly recognize accomplishments and work anniversaries. At this particular meeting, Matt called up Kari, a team member who was celebrating one year of working at the company. Matt asked Kari to say a few words about her experience over the last year. What she said confirms everything we're talking about here and everything we want to embody as a company.

"This last year has been life-changing," she began. "But there's one reason that stands out from everything else. Recently, my kids told me that over the last year, I'm more present at home because I actually enjoy what I'm doing at work. That's priceless."

Kari is a perfect example of the new workforce. And if you think Kari wouldn't go above and beyond at work because she loves what she does and sees how it affects her personal life, you're lying to yourself. Having a meaningful job doesn't just impact your work productivity; it impacts all other aspects of your life.

In his masterpiece, *Good to Great*, Jim Collins captures the idea this way:

> When [what you are deeply passionate about, what you can be best in the world at, and what drives your economic engine] come together, not only does

---

15 Mjia, "Nearly 9 out of 10 Millennials" (n. 4)

your work move toward greatness, but so does your life. For, in the end, it is impossible to have a great life unless it is a meaningful life. And it is very difficult to have a meaningful life without meaningful work. Perhaps, then, you might gain that rare tranquility that comes from knowing that you've had a hand in creating something of intrinsic excellence that makes a contribution. Indeed, you might even gain that deepest of all satisfactions: knowing that your short time here on this earth has been well spent, and that it mattered.[16]

Your employees want to matter. They want to matter to you, they want to matter to their families and others, and they want to matter to the world. If you can connect their work to that desire to matter, you and your company are poised for greatness.

CHRIS AND MATT

THE IMPORTANCE OF HIGH-PERFORMING TEAMS

Before we go any further, let's take a minute to unpack the idea of high-performing teams. We've mentioned it a few times already, and it's important. As Matt said in the introduction, your organization's goal must be to create high-performing teams. High-performing teams are what's going to make you successful.

---

16 Jim Collins, Good to Great: Why Some Companies Make the Leap . . . and Others Don't (New York: Harper Business, 2001), 210.

Remember the diagram from the introduction? Here it is again:

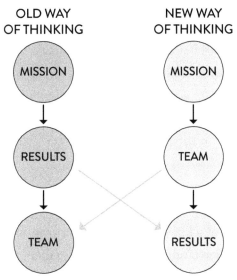

This may seem obvious, but it needs to be said: The only way you're going to get a high-performing team that produces lasting, consistent results is by focusing on the team. If your goal is to get to know and develop them, the results will naturally follow.[17] But focus on the results instead of the team, and you'll get neither.[18] When you invest in your people, they level up. That's when you hit the sales numbers, the incredible market share, and the stock launch. High-performing teams are the backbone of your company, and leadership is the backbone of high-performing teams.

A few years ago, we created a little booklet at Leader that we think helps frame everything we've talked about up to this point. So just in case you need more convincing, here's the summary from that handout that underscores what a high-performing team is and why they are important.

---

17 Of course the caveat to this is that it assumes your business model and what you're delivering is something the market wants. If you're trying to sell sand in a desert, it doesn't matter how great of a leader you are or how high-performing your team is, it just isn't going to work. Product-market fit is important.

18 Are you able to get some results doing it the other way? Sure. But you won't get them as consistently, and you won't be able to keep good people around that set you up for long-term success.

WHAT IS A HIGH-PERFORMING TEAM?

Work teams are an essential part of the modern workplace. But simply gathering a group of people together and assigning them a common goal does not create a high-performing team. High-performing teams share a commitment to their goal, but they also share a commitment to each other. Each member of a high-performing team understands their responsibilities and how their individual strengths contribute to their end goals.

High-performing teams have an exceptionally high level of trust and accountability. They encourage one another, communicate openly and honestly, and resolve conflict quickly. Within a high-performing team, there is clarity on the mission and understanding of different members' roles and responsibilities.

WHY ARE HIGH-PERFORMING TEAMS IMPORTANT?

As hybrid and remote work has risen in popularity, the need for high-performing teams has increased. The possibility that teams might be distributed across different time zones or even different countries means that the communication and collaboration that are hallmarks of high-performing teams are even more important.

Developing high-performing teams provides benefits in increased productivity and profitability. A Gallup poll found that high-performing, connected teams demonstrated a 21% increase in profitability.

Other studies have found that high-performing teams create a more enjoyable workplace. Open, honest communication and conflict resolution create a positive environment that people want to be a part of.[19]

---

19 "The Five Foundations of a High-Performing Team" Leadr, https://www.leadr.com/hubfs/eBooks/leadr-five-foundations.pdf

CHRIS

THE CAVEAT

There's an important caveat to the discussion of high-performing teams, however. You may be reading this and asking, "OK, guys, I hear what you're saying. But what happens if I have people on my team who are truly better than me, who may know more about something than I do? Are you saying I can never hope to lead them?"

That's a critical question. The short answer is no. Just because you're not the most talented person in your company or even on your team doesn't mean you can't lead people who may be.

Leading and leveling up don't come down to talent and knowledge. That's a mirage. In my relationship with Matt, for example, I have never been a VP of sales. I'm not great at cold calls. I'm not great at being in the weeds and picking out the specific reasons why a salesperson might not be hitting their goals. But I am good at creating a framework and game plan for Matt to be successful and have the freedom to do what he's best at. And I can hold him to that.

Let me put it this way: I am a mirror for Matt. That's what I was at Pushpay, and that's what I am at Leadr. In his interactions with me, I help him see what he's doing well, what he needs to improve on, and how he might be able to do it better. I ask tough questions, dig into the pain points, and encourage him when he absolutely nails it. I'm not more talented than him at sales, but I can still lead him. I can still give him the tools he needs to be better.

Think about it this way. In his prime, no one was better at golf than Tiger Woods. He was unstoppable and untouchable. And yet Tiger Woods had a golf coach. Why? Is it because his golf coach was better at golf than him? Absolutely not. It was because Tiger needed someone to hold up a mirror, someone that understood the game and could offer tips, advice, and encouragement.

If you're a manager, you're a coach. You get to hold up a mirror to those under you and guide them, develop them. And that doesn't hinge on you being more talented than the person you're coaching. It's the same thing with Bill Belichick and Tom Brady. In no world can Belichick throw a ball better than Brady. But he can coach him and create a framework and game plan for Brady to use his talents and be successful.

Think back to Matt's Nigel story. The team never complained that Nigel didn't know or understand sales. They complained that he didn't care and that he had created a poor framework and game plan for them to succeed.

Every successful team member needs someone outside of themselves and their role to be an objective observer who can help them see their blind spots. Part of leveling up as a leader means understanding and embracing that. That's why it's not just about raw talent. You can lead those more skilled than you because, in the end, talent is just one part of leadership. That's also why not every great quarterback can become a successful coach. Bart Starr was the greatest quarterback of his era, yet he fell flat when he became coach of the Green Bay Packers. Why? Because skill and leadership are different.

Ultimately, being a great leader is about understanding concepts, not necessarily being the best at them. When Matt became VP of sales at Pushpay, he wasn't necessarily the top performer. He was good, for sure. But what I saw in Matt was his ability to understand the environment and game plan and then coach those under him. The idea that you can't coach people unless you are the best at doing it is a false assumption. I've never been a marketing director, for example, but I can speak into marketing campaigns and coach my marketing people because I understand where we need to go. That's important.

Now, that said, talented people will rise to the top. And good managers enable those people, not stifle them.

There's a quote I love. I'm not sure where I heard it, but it goes like this, "Hire people who could one day take your job." Why? Because in the long run, it's good for them, it's good for the business, but it's also good for you. Think of it this way, if you surround yourself with people who could one day take your job, your job actually gets easier.

Imagine if you had an entire team of high performers that you were leading. They're hitting or exceeding goals, meeting or beating deadlines, and innovating and making everyone around them better. Do you think that makes you look good or bad? Do you think that frees you up or bogs you down? Do you think that makes your job easier or harder? You and I know the answer to those questions. Encouraging those you lead to do and be better than you is a rising tide that floats all boats – including your boat. By training people who could do your job, you're freeing yourself up to take on other challenges or opportunities in the business. The more they can do for you, the more mental space you'll have to tackle other important projects.

All of this isn't to say that the Law of the Lid doesn't apply. It does. Natural talent and ability aren't the only things, but they are some things. Just because Bill Belichick may not be able to throw like Tom Brady, that doesn't mean you could easily mimic the success Belichick and Brady had together because you're less talented than Brady as well. In the end, Belichick has a higher football IQ than maybe any coach in history, and that IQ means he is much better at leading Brady than you or I could ever be. Belichick's leadership ability is a 10, even if he can't throw a football over a mountain.[20] And that matters.

John Maxwell's words are important here: "By raising your leadership ability—

---

20 That's a Napoleon Dynamite reference for you.

without necessarily increasing your success dedication at all—you can increase your original effectiveness a tremendous amount. That's because leadership has a multiplying effect."[21]

"Leadership has a multiplying effect" sums up everything here. When you embrace that concept, you have unlocked the first key to creating high-performing teams and turboing your business.

CHRIS AND MATT

RELATIONSHIPS MATTER

So why all this talk about Nigel, mission, coaching, and the Law of the Lid? Because, in the end, a lack of leadership is a high-performing team killer. Quiet quitting is a high-performing team killer. And high-performing teams are built on people who go above and beyond and leaders who are constantly leveling up.

In other words, people check out – they 'quiet quit' – when they don't have a mission they believe in and when the Nigels of the world lead them.

Don't be a Nigel.

But how do you not become a Nigel? How do you ensure a Nigel doesn't prevent or tear down your high performers? We're glad you asked. It's not just about working for a company that embodies a solid mission, although that's important. It actually goes beyond just leveling up as a manager, although that's important, too. The surefire way to build and protect a high-performing team is for managers to develop relationships with their employees.

When you get to know your people and truly listen to them, that's the only way

---

21 Maxwell, "The Law of the Lid." (no. 3)

you can get them to rally around a mission, go above and beyond, and become a high-performing team. In fact, relationships are at the heart of everything we do. When we talk about developing people, that can only happen in the context of trust and relationships. Relationships are critical to building the five foundations we presented in the introduction. Here they are again:

- Recognizing Unique Strengths
- Personalized Growth Plans
- Setting Clear Goals
- 1-on-1 Meetings
- Giving Effective Feedback

These principles will become the basis for the next chapters of this book, but you need to know beforehand that all of them assume that you will grow as a leader by developing relationships with those underneath you.

No relationships, no success.

Suppose you are willing to partner with your employees instead of managing them, for all the reasons we've seen so far. In that case, you will experience higher performance, higher engagement, and higher retention. You will find success. And that is why you're reading this now.

CHAPTER 2

PEOPLE DEVELOPMENT

MATT

When I think about high performers, the name that comes to mind is Brittany.

Brittany was one of our most successful sales development representatives, or SDRs, at Leadr. She was on a team that specialized in prospecting, and she was absolutely crushing it. She not only beat every goal, she exceeded it. If there were a poster of the ideal employee in the breakroom, Brittany's face would have been on it. We were lucky to have her.

So I'll never forget the day she walked into her manager's office and said she was leaving. She wanted to move to Seattle to be closer to family. On top of that, she had also found a job that paid her twice as much.

When I heard the news, I was crushed. I didn't want to lose her. But after getting over the initial surprise, a thought popped into my head: this was a good thing. Yes, a "good" thing.

So I put aside my disappointment and celebrated her decision.

I didn't berate her. I didn't guilt-trip her. I didn't even try to make her stay. Instead, I told her that if she ever needed a letter of recommendation, I would be honored to write it.

Why that response? Because the role Brittany had secured, coupled with the move closer to family, was truly best for her. Sure, I would have loved for her to stay. But if I genuinely believe in – and practice – people development, then there are going to be times when, after developing someone, it's actually a good thing for them to move on. See, at the time, we didn't have a promotion available. And if Brittany stayed, two things might happen. First, she actually might regress because she had outgrown her role. Second, her deep, inner desire to be closer to family would eventually win out. At best, her performance would take a hit, and at worst, she might grow to resent us and her job.

I didn't want any of that to happen.

So I told her how incredible she was and celebrated her on the way out the door, not in a "don't-let-the-door-hit-you-on-the-way-out" way, but in every good way possible.

You want to know what she did? She went on to tell people how great it had been to work for Leadr. She became an ambassador for our company, and we hired several more great employees based on her recommendations.

In the end, the situation was a win for everyone. It was a win for Brittany because she advanced her career, and it was a win for us because she went out and told all her friends how great an experience it was working at Leadr. And, during her year at Leadr, we also benefited tremendously from how fulfilled she was while she was here.

Do you think if we had put the full-court press on Brittany to stay, she would have been as effective? No way. Because, even though we could have backed up the money truck to keep her, as we've shown up to this point, it isn't just about the money. Brittany was a young eagle who needed to soar to new heights, and it was time to let her fly. And remember, of her reasons for leaving, money was a factor, but it wasn't the only factor. Being close to family was important. So even if we gave her more money and she decided to stay, that monetary incentive would only last so long before her deeper desires took over. And when they did, we would have been left scrambling to fill her role.

A SHIFT IN THINKING

I could tell you more stories just like Brittany's. So what's the point? Well, people development requires a shift in thinking. Traditionally, as we mentioned in the introduction, companies and managers treated their employees like servants. The manager and the company wanted to squeeze every last bit of service and productivity out of an employee in the hopes that the money and desire for a job would make them stay. The employee hung on not because they wanted to but because they had to. And in the old job market, that worked.

But in today's job market, that won't cut it. Employees have way more options available to them than ever before. So when they get fed up, bored, or burned out, they move on. If you try to operate the old way in this new era, you will be bogged down with high turnover, skyrocketing costs, and low employee ROI (not to mention low morale).

When I say that employees have more options these days, I'm not making that up. Consider this: The average American will now have 12 jobs in their lifetime. Gone are the days of securing a job out of high school or college and staying there until retirement. And before you brush that off as a "Millennial" or "Gen Z" problem, the average age for someone to make a "major change" in career is 39 years old.[22] These aren't just "young people" you can write off as never being satisfied. They're the core of the new workforce.

---

22 Elsie Boskamp, "21 Crucial Career Change Statistics [2023]: How Often Do People Change Jobs?" Zippia, February 2023. https://www.zippia.com/advice/career-change-statistics/

In order, then, to get employees to stay for any length of time, you have to invest in them and develop them. In fact, you have to do that just to get them to show up nowadays. But when you do, you have to be prepared for them to move on. That's not a bad thing.

You might be reading this right now thinking, "Matt, are you saying I have to not only be OK with losing my best people but actually prepare them to leave?"

In many ways, yes! And that's where the shift in thinking comes in. If you become good at developing people, you will lose some of them because your company can never hold on to all its high performers. But can I tell you something? If you're losing people because you're so good at developing them and you have so many high performers that you can't find a place for the up-and-coming ones, that's an excellent problem to have. That actually shows how much you're nailing it.

CHRIS AND MATT

THE NICK SABAN DILEMMA

There's another football analogy that works really well here. It will help you understand why losing some people after you develop them isn't something to fear.

Nick Saban has turned the Alabama Crimson Tide football team into a perennial powerhouse. He's led his Alabama teams to six national championships, 15 bowl game victories, nine SEC West titles, and eight SEC championships. On top of that, from 2012 to 2021, he had the best recruiting class in eight out of those ten years.[23] He's not just dominated on the field, but he's dominated off of it when it comes to securing the best talent.

---

23 Dustin Schutte, "Graphic Shows How Dominant Alabama Has Been on the Recruiting Front for the Last Decade." Saturday Tradition, 2021. https://saturdaytradition.com/big-ten-football/graphic-shows-how-dominant-alabama-has-been-on-the-recruiting-front-for-the-last-decade/

But do you know what that means? There are a lot of highly-touted recruits and only 22 starting spots. In Saban's world, he's investing in young athletes – developing them, so to speak – and yet there's not room for everyone on the team.

Let's put it this way: Nick Saban is so excellent at what he does that his backups are good enough to be starters elsewhere. You can guess what happens, then. Many highly-touted recruits he invests in and develops eventually leave to go elsewhere. They transfer out.

"When a roster is made up almost entirely of blue-chip talent, there simply aren't enough available snaps to go around," writes Alabama football blogger Zach Breathwaite. "Former 4-star and even 5-star recruits are forced to seek greener pastures when they are beat out by better players."

He continues: "As a result, Alabama football typically sees an offseason exodus of transfers. This has always been the case under Coach Saban, and the emergence of the transfer portal has only accelerated the process of weeding out those that aren't destined to finish their careers in Tuscaloosa."[24]

How many athletes transfer out of Alabama? In the offseason between 2021 and 2022, the team saw 20 players look for opportunities elsewhere. That's a high number, especially compared to its rivals.

But let us ask you a question: Does that show how good or bad Saban is at his job? The obvious answer is that it shows he's not only good at his job, he's the best at it![25]

It's the same concept we're trying to drive home here. You losing people to

---

24 Zach Breathwaite, "Alabama Football and Its Unique Relationship With the Transfer Portal." Bamahammer, August 2022. https://bamahammer.com/2022/08/16/alabama-football-transfer-portal/

25 An important caveat: The reason why stars are transferring out matters. If your team is awful, your coach is bad, and there's no chemistry, a high amount of transfers is an indication of something bad, not something good.

better opportunities because you've developed them is a case study of why this new approach works. It doesn't reflect poorly on you, but rather the opposite.[26]

You need to be the Nick Saban of your business. Coach your people well, invest in them, and develop them. In turn, they will work hard and put their whole selves into what they're doing, and you'll have national championships as a result. And if you can't promote those people – either because you don't have the room or because your roster is already filled with 5-star recruits – you should celebrate them on their way out, knowing that you've made their lives better and they've given you everything they have while with you. Once again, that's not a bad thing.

Does that mean you never try and get them to stay? Absolutely not. When it makes sense, you should have a conversation with a transferring employee about their dreams and goals. Maybe there's a chance, with some patience and creativity, that your organization might still be the right fit. But if, at the end of that conversation, it's obvious that either you can't give them what they need, that they have a better opportunity elsewhere, or that there is no benefit to, say, them delaying their departure for a possible opportunity in your company further down the road, then letting them go is the best thing for them and the best thing for you.

You better believe Nick Saban is having that type of conversation with a 5-star quarterback recruit who's stuck behind the starter for the foreseeable future and wants to transfer to Western Kentucky, where he can plug in as the immediate QB1. But the reality is that if you've done things right, you will face the Nick Saban dilemma. And it's a good problem to have.

---

26 Again, the caveat here is that you have to understand why people are leaving. Don't take a look at your turnover rate and start doing cartwheels automatically if it's high. It has to be high for the right reasons!

CHRIS

The Nick Saban example is a good one, but I want to add something else. When a manager asks me, "What if I develop my people and they still leave?" I like to flip it around and ask them, "What if you don't develop your people, and they stay?" I also follow it up with, "What's more important and healthy for your team?" Inevitably, the manager admits that it's better to develop their employees and risk them leaving than it is to not develop them and have them stay.

Let me be as clear as possible: If you don't have opportunities for high performers to stay within your organization, then some of them will leave. But that's preferable to not developing them and filling your company with a bunch of average employees.

Again, this is a shift in thinking. But it's a shift in thinking that's backed up by data about this new workforce and this new era of employer-employee relationships. Remember, the days of someone joining your company and staying for 15 years are over. If you expect to keep your employees forever, you need to give up on that. It's done. That's not gonna happen anymore.

The average worker aged 25-34 – which is currently the backbone of the new workforce – stays at a job for just over three years.[27] Do I think that if you develop people, you can increase that average? Absolutely. We wouldn't be writing this book if we didn't think so. But we also want you to be realistic. And the reality is that employees are changing jobs more frequently now than ever. That means you can either put in place a robust development plan for your employees and risk losing some high performers, or you can sit on your hands and watch them leave anyway. If you do that, if you refuse to develop them, then you're missing out on the incredible benefits they could bring you during their tenure at your organization.

---

27 "17 Remarkable Career Change Statistics to Know." Apollo Technical, December 2022. https://www.apollotechnical.com/career-change-statistics/

Think about this: We had Brittany for just over a year at Leadr. Eighteen months, to be specific. That's not a long time. And yet, because we invested in her and she blossomed, we got more dedication and hard work in that short time than we've gotten from some people who stuck with us for five years. In the end, Brittany wanted to move closer to her family. There's nothing that we could have done to retain her where she would be happy, fulfilled, and sustained long term.

But let me say this: In my experience, for every high performer we developed at Pushpay, and at Leadr, that we celebrated on the way out because we didn't have a place to plug them in, there are two more that we could and did find a place for.

Listen, people are going to leave. That's the reality of this job market. And as we mentioned, it's a natural byproduct of you developing people well. As a leader, the best thing you can do is create a system that continues to develop high performers, plugs people in where you can, and treats the others well on their way out.

You'll reap the immediate benefits of their productivity and the future benefits when those people become apostles for you, as Brittany did for us.

CHRIS AND MATT

"THE ALLIANCE"

We understand this shift from people development to people management is a new idea and requires a different way of thinking. And while we've covered it in several ways up to this point, we think it's important to really drill down on the idea before we go any further.

The best summary of this new way of thinking comes from a New York Times bestseller, *The Alliance* by Reid Hoffman. Hoffman is the co-founder and former chairman of LinkedIn.

Some of this will sound familiar to what we've covered so far in this book, but we think it will help to hear it summarized differently.

At the core of Hoffman's seminal work on the topic is the idea that employers and employees come together in a loosely made, mutually beneficial bargain. (Sound familiar?) There are clear terms and expectations (which we'll get into in later chapters). The employer gets to know the employee, understands where he or she wants to go, and then invests in that employee. Feeling heard, validated, and fulfilled, the employee offers his or her talents and passion to move the company forward.

In other words, the employer and employee make "an alliance" and agree to collaborate. Both parties derive value from that agreement because both are invested (a key word) in each other's success.

That's where people development comes in. This bargain, this alliance, isn't possible in the people management world; it's only possible if you adopt a people development mindset. However, there's a key element involved in all of this – both in the alliance and in people development – that we haven't talked about much: trust. Trust is the foundation of people development, the alliance, and company health in general. And both the employer and the employee must feel and embody it.

Hoffman sums it up nicely (while also giving a nod to the idea that, like we've been saying, the workforce has changed):

As much as companies might yearn for a stable environment and employees might yearn for lifetime employment, the world has irrevocably changed. But we also can't keep going the way we've been going. Trust in the business world (as measured by the proportion of employees who say they have a "high level of trust in management and the organization" they work for) is near an all-time low. A business without loyalty is a business without long-term thinking. A business without long-term thinking is a business that's unable to invest in the future. And a business that isn't investing in tomorrow's opportunities and technologies—well, that's a company already in the process of dying.[28]

In other words, people development requires trust.

Now, the temptation for you as a manager is to say, "Yeah, you're right. I need to be able to trust that if I invest in this employee, he or she won't take advantage of me and walk out the door at the first opportunity to get more money."

Once again, that's the old way of thinking. That's not trust. You, as a manager, need to model trust first. If you want to be trusted, you have to find ways to show your trust to those around you and under you. You must show your employees that you are a person of your word. You need to give respect to get respect.

It all starts with trust. And trust starts with you.

And in case you want to know how important trust is, consider this: One survey found that 65% of employees would rather have their boss fired than get a raise.[29] You better believe that's because of a lack of trust. In other words, if you don't build trust with your employees, they'd rather see you fired than make more money. That's staggering.

---

28 Reid Hoffman, Ben Casnocha, Chris Yeh, The Alliance: Managing Talent in the Networked Age (Boston: Harvard Business Review Press, 2014), 7.

29 Meghan Casserly, "Majority of Americans Would Rather Fire Their Boss Than Get a Raise." Forbes, October 2012. https://www.forbes.com/sites/meghancasserly/2012/10/17/majority-of-americans-would-rather-fire-their-boss-than-get-a-raise/

That said, we want to take a quick break from speaking to leaders and speak directly to the employees reading this book. As an employee, you might be tempted to think, "Yeah! You need to make me happy. Management is dead. Leave me alone, and let me do my thing!"

But that's not being an employee or a teammate. That's being an independent contractor. People development only works if you, as the employee, are just as bought into the alliance as your manager.

Just like the alliance doesn't let the leader off the hook, it also doesn't let the employee off the hook either. You have to uphold your end of the bargain and perform. You have to be invested. You have to be active.

If you feel micromanaged, for example, the alliance concept says you need to help your leader become more of a developer and less of a manager by proactively communicating. You need to think like an owner. You need to bring ideas and solutions to the table. And most importantly, you need to follow through on the job the company hired you to do.

That's what contributing looks like – what fulfilling your side of the bargain looks like. An alliance takes at least two parties to work. It's never one-sided.

HIRING ENTREPRENEURS

The alliance, however, presupposes something else important: adopting new hiring practices. If there's an old way of thinking, then there's also an old way of hiring.

In the old way of hiring, you looked for people with clearly-defined skills. You didn't hire people; you hired their resumes. You had a specific need, and then you looked for people who fit that need. That's one of the byproducts of the industrial revolution. People were assembly line workers, and they could be plugged in and replaced at a moment's notice.

But we live in an era of the tech revolution. Jobs aren't plug-and-play anymore. People aren't cogs in a wheel or warm bodies on an assembly line. They aren't tied to a factory or even an office. They have dreams, goals, and visions. They want to feel you care about them and where they are headed. As we discussed earlier, everyone has a "side hustle" these days because they want to do meaningful work.

What does that mean? It means you must search for people who want more than to be a cog. You want people who will fight, tooth and nail, to be better. You want people who look at your job posting and say, "I can do that. But I can also do so much more. I want to do so much more."

Hire people with an entrepreneurial bent.

Do they need to have the right skills for the job you're hiring for? Absolutely. But there are more important things than making sure someone knows how to make a call, code an email, or design a presentation. You need them to care, and the best way to get people to care is to have their buy-in. And you get their buy-in by tapping into their entrepreneurial spirit – that innate desire to create and build.

Your goal, then, should be to hire people who want to create and build, and then invest so heavily in them that they want to create and build for you. That's the key. Sure, you can hire people who just want to punch a clock. But then you'll only ever get clock-punchers.

Listen, every organization needs people willing to do the actual hard work. Yours does, too. So we're not saying that every role in your organization needs to be filled with dreamers. But we will say this: We'd take a dreamer willing to spend a season assembling widgets any day over someone whose ceiling is simply a widget assembler. You can go to new heights with the former, but you'll be stuck in place with the latter. You need more dreamers than you realize.

And the data says that now, more than ever, dreamers and entrepreneurs are on the rise, especially in a post-COVID world. According to census numbers, there were 5.4 million small business applications in 2021. That's a 53% increase from 2019 pre-pandemic levels.[30] In other words, COVID awakened many people's entrepreneurial spirit. That means you have a much larger pool to choose from now.

"People are looking for working arrangements that are more suitable to how they want to live their lives," Steven Davis, an economist at the University of Chicago Booth School of Business, explains regarding this data.[31] It's exactly what we've been talking about. You would be wise to use that to your advantage.

But how do you take advantage of that entrepreneurial spirit? A significant way is to change the types of questions you're asking in interviews. Ask more open-ended ones. Ask about a candidate's dreams and aspirations. Ask about what motivates them, and listen closely for clues about where they want to go. And don't be scared off if they tell you they want to start their own company someday. Hire that person immediately!

It's your job to identify the entrepreneurial-minded people, hire them, and then invest in them because they can offer you way more if you let them. In the old way of thinking and hiring, people with entrepreneurial spirits were stifled and dismissed. They disrupted. We're here to tell you that you need to not only welcome the disrupters but also intentionally seek them out.

Your company and your future depend on them.

---

30 Erica Pandey, "The Pandemic-Era Small Business Boom." Axios, February 2022. https://www.axios.com/2022/02/15/small-business-boom-covid-recession-pandemic

31 Ibid

So now that we've laid all of that out, it's time to show you not just the why but the how. How do you leave behind people management and embrace people development? How do you implement it in your company? That's where the five foundations come in.

PART 2

THE 5 FOUNDATIONS OF PEOPLE DEVELOPMENT

CHAPTER 3

RECOGNIZING UNIQUE STRENGTHS

MATT

Can I be vulnerable with you?

When I first took the job as VP of sales at Pushpay, I had no idea what I was doing. Sure, I had done sales, but I had never held a management position that high up in an organization. While I was trying my best to exude outward confidence, internally, I was insecure. Extremely insecure.

In all honesty, I felt like I was drowning.

"I'm not sure I'm the right person for this," I remember telling myself multiple times a day. After all, I was the company's fifth VP of sales in the last three years. Those aren't good odds.

Chris's confidence in me went a long way, for sure. But I was still struggling. That's why I'll never forget the conversation I had with the chairman of the board shortly after I stepped into the role.

During a visit to the Pushpay offices, the chairman called me into one of the conference rooms. I was nervous. "Was this it?" I asked myself. "Am I about to become the next casualty of this position?"

I couldn't have been more wrong.

When I entered the room, I saw him sitting across the long table from me. After some quick pleasantries, he asked a simple question: "Matt, what do you think it takes to be a great VP of sales?"

I was worried it was a trick question, that he was looking for the exact right answer, like it was a test. And who wouldn't feel that way? That's a pretty big, open-ended question. My mind started racing, and I spit out the worst possible answer.

"Well, I don't really know. I'm just trying to keep my head above water," I said.

I still roll my eyes thinking about that.

"Well, Matt, I can think of about ten things that it takes," he replied.

"Great," I thought. "Completely nailed that one!"

But instead of making me feel small, what he said next changed my life.

"You have all of them," he said.

I wish I could share a video of my face at that moment with you. To say I was shocked is an understatement.

"Excuse me?" I said.

"You heard me," he responded, not dismissively but confidently. "You have all of them. I'm not looking for someone that's been doing this for 15 years. I'm looking for someone that can grow into the role. My ten criteria have nothing to do with direct skills. You can learn that stuff. But at the core of who you are, you have the ability to do this role. I know you well enough to say that. I've seen your strengths. You're the right person for this job."

And that was it. The conversation lasted maybe 15 minutes. I was almost speechless. I stood up and walked away with all the confidence in the world. My whole demeanor changed. After all, my boss's boss just told me that I meet all the criteria he's looking for in a VP of sales, knowing full well that I had my fair share of weaknesses.

I thought I hadn't proven that I could do the role. But apparently, I had been proving it all along.

CALLING OUT POTENTIAL

I learned something valuable from the chairman that day: There's a difference between skills and strengths.

That's why the title of this chapter is so crucial. It's "Recognizing Unique Strengths," not "Recognizing Unique Skills." When it comes to developing your people, one of your most important jobs is focusing on strengths over skills. Here's the difference: Skills are all about the here and now, the immediate; strengths are all about potential, the future. If you want to move your company forward, you must think about potential just as much, if not more, than whatever trumped-up "skills" someone puts on a resume. Because, in the end, people will stretch the truth as much as possible on a resume.

All of that brings me to Jay.

I met Jay a few years ago. He became a best-selling author with his debut book. Before that, he was an influential journalist. His writing has appeared in some of the most popular publications and websites out there. But guess what: He didn't go to school for journalism. He didn't go to school for creative writing. Among other things, he studied economics and philosophy in college.

So how does someone who didn't study writing become a prolific writer?

"My degree required a lot of critical thinking and learning how to convey and convince others of what I believed," he once told me. "What I learned in college was how to take big concepts, and what was going on in my head, and put them into words. And then I had people along the way who called that strength out in me and helped me develop the individual skills after."

"College taught me how the world works," he added, "but I discovered – through plenty of encouragement from others – I had the core ability to take that information and write about it in a way that was easy for others to understand and grasp."

That's a great example of what we're talking about here. Recognizing strengths is about identifying potential. That's what the chairman did with me. And it's what others did with Jay.

Let me say this: If someone has the foundational strengths, the potential, they can learn the necessary skills. But it's much harder to manufacture strengths than it is to teach skills.

In my situation, I could learn how to make budgets, conduct effective reviews, and give quarterly presentations. But the problem with many of the previous people who held my role was that they possessed the skills that look good on a resume but lacked the core leadership strengths that would actually make them effective leaders.

Our chairman wasn't calling out unique competencies and skills in me. He was calling out my capacity to do great things based on my strength and potential that not even I saw in myself. When you do the same, when you recognize your team's unique strengths, you'll not only help them unlock their hidden potential but also your company's hidden potential.

Is that going to be frustrating at times? You bet. There are times it will feel like you care and believe more in your employee than even they do. But that's leadership. When you believe in someone more than they believe in themselves, it brings them, it brings you, and it brings the company to a higher level. In the end, I'd rather assume the best in someone and be wrong than assume the worst and be right.

Let me give you a practical example of what this looks like. I've found that people often limit themselves because they don't know how far they can stretch their abilities. As a leader, you need to find ways to nudge them toward stretching themselves and self-sufficiency. You need to empower them.

The best way to do this is with two simple words: You decide. Think about how empowering those words are. I once heard someone say that those were a leader's two most powerful words.

Here's what this looks like in reality.

I once had an employee, let's call her Sally. Sally worked hard, was highly driven, and wanted to do her very best.

The problem was, because previous managers she'd worked with didn't empower her or recognize her strengths, Sally had relegated herself to being an order-taker. Most of our conversations would start with her asking, "What would you like me to do?" Or, "What should I do here?" She was scared to make her own decisions, scared to try things, and scared to fail or make mistakes. Because of that, she wasn't growing. I could see her unique strengths and knew she had the capacity to do more, but she was stunting her own growth.

Here's the other thing: Your organization moves very slowly when you, as the leader, are the bottleneck for all decisions. So after a few weeks of Sally asking me to make decisions for her, I started responding with those two powerful words: "You decide."

Sally was stumped. Initially, she tried another route by saying, "Well, what would you do if you were me?"

I wasn't going to let her off the hook. "Nope. You decide," I said.

Quickly, she realized what I was doing, took the reins, and started getting things done without having to check in with me on everything. And slowly but surely, after several "you decide" conversations, she became a self-starter instead of an order-taker. She and the company were better off for it.

That's what it looks like to recognize strengths and empower your people. Do you know what else that does? It builds trust, which we explored as a key principle in the last chapter. And trust is going to pay dividends throughout your organization.

THE IMPORTANCE OF WEAKNESSES

I hate personality tests. OK, maybe "hate" is too strong of a word, but I struggle with them. Here's why: They focus too much on what a person does well and not enough on what they do poorly.

"But Matt, you just told me I had to focus on a person's strengths!"

You're right. I just spent a lot of time telling you about focusing on strengths. But that doesn't mean you ignore the weaknesses. In fact, if you want to develop people, you have to understand their weaknesses. People development is as much about weaknesses as it is about strengths.

Back to personality assessments. The Enneagram is the latest, in-vogue personality assessment. I've taken it. You've likely taken it. I think a lot of people have. It gives you a number and then unpacks what that number means about you.

A 1 is "The Reformer," which is described as someone who is purposeful, principled, and self-controlled. A 2 is "The Helper," and so on, up to the number 9. In our business, we see a lot of 8s. Those are the people who are generally the alphas. They're straight shooters. They take the bull by the horns, so to speak.

But here's the thing. Too many people who take the Enneagram, or any type of personality test, use it to excuse their behavior instead of change it. I can't tell you how many times I've talked to someone about their tone or actions and heard, "Yeah, but it's because I'm an 8."

No, it's because you're a jerk.

In other words, people use the Enneagram and other personality tests to dismiss and explain away their weaknesses instead of working on them.

And I can't blame them. For years we've been taught to only focus on our strengths. But that mentality is killing businesses, and it's not people development. Sure, we need to double down on what people do well.

That's natural. But if you ignore someone's weaknesses, they're never going to truly and fully develop, you're never going to get all you can out of them, and you're actually doing them a disservice.

Here's the thing: No one can afford to have big, gaping weaknesses in their life. You know this inherently if you're married or in a committed relationship. Imagine you went to your partner and said, "Honey, I know I really stink at communicating my feelings. But I'm really good at budgeting and finances. So I'm just going to ignore my lack of communication and be the best finance manager for the house that I can be." That relationship would never last.

Similarly, I once had an employee – a manager underneath me – who I asked to put together a budget. We got to the point where we were going to go over it, and when we sat down, it was absolutely awful. When I asked him about it, he responded, "Well, I'm just not a numbers guy."

"You can't afford not to be a numbers guy if you're going to make it here or anywhere else," I told him.

There's an old idea that goes something like this: "Work on your weaknesses and become average. Work on your strengths and become exceptional."

There's a danger with this approach, however. For example, I hear this a lot concerning public speaking. We mentioned earlier in the book that we regularly do company-wide meetings to talk about goals and progress and to recognize accomplishments. During that time, we often ask different people to speak. And there have been plenty of times when someone has said, "I'd rather not. I'm not really good at public speaking."

You know what my response is? "You're capping your growth if you don't practice it. If you want to be in leadership, you can't afford not to be good, or at least proficient, in public speaking."

Here's the point: Recognizing unique strengths is not an excuse to ignore weaknesses. Again, you are doing your employees – and yourself – a disservice if you do that. People development is definitely about recognizing strengths, but it's also about turning weaknesses into strengths, or at least competencies.

That's what the chairman was getting at that day in the conference room. Did I have hiccups after that conversation? You better believe it. But we worked on them; we didn't ignore them. Remember, we both understood that I had growing to do and that I struggled in certain areas. He recognized my core strengths, and then his assumption was we would work on my weaknesses.

The head of marketing at Leadr and I regularly joke about this. She's a big fan of the Enneagram. But the point I always make is that we have to recognize and work on our weaknesses, and personality tests tend to give us an excuse not to do that.

In fact, you could also say that personality tests tend to pigeonhole us into strengths as well. Enneagram 8s tend not to be empathetic, for example. But leaders need to understand and learn empathy. Yet too many 8s think that can never be a strength because, well, 8s aren't really empathetic.

That's horrible and dangerous thinking.

We'll talk more about how to give feedback about weaknesses to your employees in Chapter 7, but let me sum part of it up here: You don't have to be a jerk (especially just because you're an 8). But the foundational point is that you and your company can't afford not to help your people work on their weaknesses. And you, personally, can't afford to take that approach either.

Don't let someone's strengths mask their weaknesses, or at least don't let their strengths give them an excuse to ignore their weaknesses. The stakes are too high.

CHRIS

While I don't share Matt's disdain for the Enneagram, his point is a good one.

I remember vividly one day at Pushpay when we were hosting the head of HR from the wildly successful company, DocuSign. Chances are you've used DocuSign in some form to electronically sign anything from a real estate contract to a job offer.

We wanted to glean as much as we could from him, so I was peppering him with questions. One of those was, "How do you develop your people?"

His response actually planted one of the very first seeds for Leadr in my mind.

"Chris, that's a great question," he started. "Here's how you develop people: You take a list of the five biggest problems facing your business today, and you write them on a board: 1, 2, 3, 4, 5. And then, on the other side of the board, you write a list of the five highest-potential employees that you have, and you write them on the other side: 1, 2, 3, 4, 5. And then what you do is match up people with a problem, which is really an opportunity."

It was like a lightbulb went off over my head. Why? Because when it comes to people development, it's as much about stretching and growing your people out of their weaknesses as it is about handing them tasks and responsibilities you know they can crush.

There's something else significant there. In every one of my companies, I've had a library program in place. That means anyone who wants to advance themselves can buy a book, write a one-page summary, submit it to their manager, and then be reimbursed for the cost of the book. That's because, traditionally, I've believed that you grow by reading books. That is still true to a certain extent, but what the DocuSign executive taught me is that you really, truly grow by putting what you learn (or read about) into practice – by being stretched in real-world situations and scenarios.

In other words, you grow the most by doing. Think of it this way: If you want to grow your muscles, you have to lift something that's a little too heavy. Your muscles stretch - tear, really - and then when they grow back, they're stronger. It's the same with your business muscles. If increasing your strength is the process of breaking down and rebuilding your muscles, you have to find challenges that do that to you professionally. You have to be outside of your comfort zone to be able to grow and develop as a person.

So here's the question you need to ask yourself: How am I challenging myself and those under me? It's impossible to answer that question without knowing both your strengths and weaknesses and theirs.

Here's an example. Let's say you have a massive problem with sales and marketing. You might approach an employee, let's call her Danika, and say something like, "Danika, you are the highest capacity individual that I have. I need you to be the owner of this problem and opportunity. If you take this on and nothing happens, then it's not a big deal because we didn't expect a miracle. But if you solve it, you'll reach your potential a lot quicker."

If Danika takes that opportunity and delivers on it, it's a massive win for the business, and it's a massive win for her. And by giving the problem to a high-performing individual, you have your best chance of actually solving the problem.

Now I know we reiterated this in earlier chapters, but I need to do it again here.

Some of you still struggle with the old way of thinking: "What if I do what you just said, Chris, and the person I entrust outshines me or becomes even better than me?"

There's a concept here that you can't forget. The fastest way to get promoted is to get your boss promoted. What I mean by that is if you give people opportunities to grow and they crush it, once again, you're actually setting yourself up for more success. Do you think your boss will look at you with disdain because you were able to put in place a game plan for figuring out a massive problem? Or do you think your boss will be happy and proud of what you just did, even if you weren't responsible for the direct work?

You and I both know it's the second one.

It reminds me of a great quote by Zig Ziglar. "You can have everything in life you want, if you will just help enough other people get what they want."

If by understanding your employees' strengths and weaknesses, you are solving problems and the business is growing and winning, good things will happen for you and those around you.

Once again, that frees you up to do more of what matters, like anticipating bigger issues. If you, as a manager, are constantly trying to solve every problem, that means you're not looking ahead. You're dropping the ball on one of the most important aspects of being a leader: seeing what's coming next and preparing for it. That's why you need to enable those under you to do their jobs well and stretch them so that you can focus on the next mile, the next five miles, the next 10 miles ahead.

I've met too many managers who are so focused on the day-to-day, so bogged down by the problems of the here and now, that they never get a chance to focus on what actually moves the needle. You have to carve out time to start thinking about moving your team, your division, and your company forward. And you'll never be able to do that if you don't stretch the people below you.

In the end, that's what happened with Matt when I gave him an opportunity to solve our sales woes. I didn't come up with the plan that turned things around. I asked him to. I knew he was a high-performing team member, so I presented him with the problem. He was empowered to come up with a solution, and then I gave him the reins to execute that plan.

It worked. All because I saw his strengths and weaknesses and then allowed him the opportunity to stretch himself.

CHRIS AND MATT

PERSONALITY AND STRENGTH ASSESSMENTS

One final note on personality and strength assessments: Even though Matt may be skeptical of how the Enneagram is used, that doesn't mean it's useless. We have found many benefits in having our employees take a variety of tests when we hire them.

It's certainly helpful for us, but we've found it's really helpful for the employee. It forces introspection. And the best employees are the self-aware ones. There's an extreme benefit there.

In the end, as a leader, it's critical to understand that one size does not fit all when coaching each of your team members. Knowing how each individual communicates, prefers to work, and naturally learns is vital to building trust and engagement. Personality assessments help you with that. They give you a peek into the strengths and weaknesses of individuals in your organization.

Using multiple assessments can even help to paint a multi-faceted picture of your team members.

And even though we've made a point that understanding weaknesses are just as important as understanding strengths, research from Gallup has found that people who use their strengths every day are three times more likely to report having an excellent quality of life. They are six times more likely to be engaged at work. They feel 8% more productive and 15% less likely to quit their jobs.[32]

That's key.

So here's a list of the assessments we like to use:

- **The Enneagram** measures how people connect, react to, and perceive the world.
- **The DiSC** profile measures behavioral tendencies and preferences.
- **The Myers-Briggs** assessment identifies areas of strength based on a person's use of perception and judgment.
- **StrengthsFinder** and **Working Genius** highlight lists of strengths that each individual has.

To help you, we've included a more detailed look at these in Appendix A.

In the end, to develop people, you have to have knowledge. And the more knowledge you have, the better you will be and the better you can help your employees to be.

Find strengths. Grow weaknesses. Reap the rewards.

---

32 Peter Flade, Jim Asplund, and Gwen Elliot, "Employees Who Use Their Strengths Outperform Those Who Don't." Gallup, October 2015. https://www.gallup.com/workplace/236561/employees-strengths-outperform-don.aspx#:~:text=-Gallup%20analysis%20reveals%20that%20people,likely%20to%20quit%20their%20jobs.

CHAPTER 4

PERSONALIZED GROWTH PLANS

MATT

Remember Brittany, our high-performing sales development representative from Chapter 2? We need to talk a little bit more about her.

While at Leadr, Brittany was hungry to grow. That continued throughout her entire tenure with us, but there was a particular meeting I had with her early on that set the tone.

During one of our first 1-on-1 meetings, she came the most prepared I've ever seen someone come to a 1-on-1. She walked into my office, sat down, and pulled out a list of 15 questions.

She must have spent at least an hour creating those questions because they were deep. They were thoughtful. They were hard. They weren't about my favorite color or even about what I thought of her performance. They were the kind of questions that keep a manager up at night.

- What motivates you?
- What keeps you working hard?

- What's it like being a CEO?
- Do you recommend I work like you do?

You can see what I mean. And even though the questions were hard, I answered them with as much candor as I could.[33] She took notes, asked follow-up questions, and sought feedback. I can honestly say it was one of the best meetings I've ever been a part of. Not the easiest, but the best.

So why do I tell you that story?

Because during that meeting, Brittany clarified why she was at Leadr, even if she never spelled it out exactly. Yes, she was here to help Leadr and make a living. But more importantly for her, she demonstrated that she was here to grow. To learn. That meeting became a huge part of kicking off what we call a personalized growth plan. And if I'm being honest, in hindsight, that meeting also immediately started the clock on her time with us. It was evident that Brittany was destined for greatness. And because of my dedication to people development, I was excited to help her get there.

She was never going to stay an SDR with meeting preparation and questions like that. Never. I knew it. She knew it. And still, we made an alliance (there's that concept again) to help each other and implemented a personalized growth plan.

And we both benefited greatly.

CHRIS AND MATT

THE IMPORTANCE OF GROWTH PLANS

By this point, you've seen that developing and retaining key talent is crucial

---

33 We'll talk more about how much is appropriate to share with an employee in Chapter 7.

to the success of your organization. The workplace has changed, especially in the last few years. Remember, today's employees want more than just increased pay or a trumped-up title. They want careers where they can learn, grow, be challenged, and be valued for the ideas they bring to the table.

Harvard Business Review found that 9 out of 10 people are willing to take less pay to do more meaningful work.[34] In fact, a study by LinkedIn found that 94% of workers would stay at a job longer if the company simply invested in their growth.[35]

Those numbers shouldn't be surprising to you by now because we've already mentioned similar ones. So why do we bring them up again? Because the way to invest in people, help them grow, and get them to stay longer is through personalized growth plans.

Still, we went back and forth on where to put this chapter in the book. Ultimately, we felt that putting it here was the best call.[36] Why? Because after you recognize someone's unique strengths, you need to formulate a personalized growth plan. It's not only a crucial step; it's the next step.

That's because, as a people developer, you need to get to know your employees. You need to really understand who they are and where they want to go. And a personalized growth plan is exactly how you do that.[37] In fact, as you'll see below, getting to know your employees is foundational to even formulating an effective, personalized growth plan.

---

34 Shawn Achor et al, "9 out of 10 People are Willing to Earn Less Money to Do More-Meaningful Work." Harvard Business Review, November 2018, https://hbr.org/2018/11/9-out-of-10-people-are-willing-to-earn-less-money-to-do-more-meaningful-work

35 Abigail Johnson Hess, "LinkedIn: 94% of Employees Say They Would Stay at a Company Longer For This Reason - And It's Not a Raise." CNBC, February 2019, https://www.cnbc.com/2019/02/27/94percent-of-employees-would-stay-at-a-company-for-this-one-reason.html

36 These foundations build off of each other. And there are a couple ways to arrange the stones in order to build your high-performing team. But what isn't debatable is that this is a foundation stone that has to be laid near the bottom.

37 The vehicle for accomplishing a personalized growth plan is the 1-1 meeting, which we'll talk about in-depth in Chapter 7.

There's a key word we're using in all of this, by the way: personalized. We mentioned this in the last chapter, but it bears repeating here: There is no one-size-fits-all development style.[38] What we mean is that every single one of your employees is an individual with individual dreams, goals, and learning styles, just to name a few. You have to take the general framework we're outlining here but then tailor it to each employee.

DEFINING A PERSONALIZED GROWTH PLAN

So what is a personalized growth plan? Great question. Before we tell you what it is, though, we have to tell you what it is not.

A personalized growth plan is not a PIP (performance improvement plan). PIPs are generally last-ditch efforts to try and salvage a floundering employee. PGPs (personalized growth plans) aren't done near the end of someone's tenure with your company. They're done near the beginning. They set the foundation because they are the foundation of the alliance we've been talking about.

In other words, you and the employee can't decide on what is mutually beneficial until you understand what the employee wants out of their job, where they want to go, and how you can help them get there. In fact, that's why we talked earlier about implementing some of the goal-oriented questions into the hiring process. By doing that, you're better set up for this step, and you can get a better idea of the potential employee's fit.

That said, a personalized growth plan can and should be worked into an employee's regular performance reviews. And in fact, it makes performance reviews that much easier because you and the employee have already set measurable goals. (More on that in the next chapter.)

---

38 Notice we didn't say "management" style there. That's very intentional.

So we'll state the question again: What is a personalized growth plan? Simply put, it's a plan that focuses on an individual's goals. It's an opportunity to explore their dreams and aspirations. The goals should be attainable and measurable and broken down into actionable steps.[39] Why is that important? Because it increases employee engagement.

We've talked about employee engagement before, but it's no coincidence that it's coming up again here. We know teams are much more likely to succeed in meeting company goals when employee engagement is a focus, leading to a significant decrease in things like turnover and absenteeism and an increase in productivity. Well, personalized growth plans are the tool to build that engagement. Overall, development programs foster new skills, encourage teamwork and collaboration, and could even help your meetings be more efficient and productive. (And who doesn't want that.)

When a growth plan is done right, it increases employee engagement.

If you find employees disengaged, unsatisfied, or leaving, you need to engage them with a personalized growth plan. And even if you don't see those issues, personalized growth plans can turbo your current high performers.

Take Brittany. If she had shown the kind of drive she did by asking the questions she did, and we didn't follow up with a personalized growth plan, we would have lost her much sooner. She would have had to move on. And that would have been our fault, not hers.

IMPLEMENTING PERSONALIZED GROWTH PLANS

So what does it look like to implement personalized growth plans? Well, at

---

39 Once again, more on goals in the next chapter. But now you see why this had to come first.

Leadr, we decided to take a unique approach. Sure, you can write down dreams and goals on a piece of paper, but that doesn't really show you take this seriously. If you want to earn your employees' trust, a key concept we've discussed, you have to show how much you value not only them but their growth.

In the end, a good manager takes an interest in their employees. A great manager takes an interest in their employees' dreams and goals. Those things should go hand in hand, but the reality is they historically haven't.

So to foster that type of relationship, we created a repeatable and sustainable growth and feedback system. It's called LeadrU, a five-month leadership development track that helps us engage and grow every member of our team. It's structured enough to bring consistency to our leadership development efforts as a company, but it also allows room for the employee to customize it to their personal growth goals.

We'll share exactly how LeadrU works here, but we want to emphasize that you have the freedom to make it unique to your own company.

LEADRU

LeadrU includes two major phases: the "prerequisites list" and the LeadrU Personal Plan.

Prerequisites List

You need buy-in from your employees on a lot of things, especially when it comes to implementing personal growth plans. That's why the first crucial step to a personalized growth plan actually rests on the employee, all with the goal of securing their buy-in. That's why we've developed a prerequisites list that the employee must complete before officially making a growth plan.

In addition to securing their buy-in, the prerequisites list allows you to really get to know your employee, which fosters relationships and trust. So, here are the steps we require our employees to take before we even get to a personalized growth plan. We've included an explanation for each:

Watch Ten Onboarding Videos

We've chosen ten videos that we consider an introduction to Leadr culture, including recordings of crucial quarterly kickoff meetings and talks from great leaders we admire and trust. Everyone is required to watch them. These videos set the tone for what employees will learn throughout their program. We encourage you to start making a list now of resources that you think are crucial for your employees to digest.

Take a "How to Work Well With Me" Survey

This survey consists of information including communication style, personal insights, likes and dislikes, what motivates them to do their best work, what demotivates them, how they show they value someone, and how they like to be shown that they're valued. This helps us connect with each employee on a personal level and understand their unique strengths and personalities. This is where the personality tests we mentioned in the last chapter can also come into play.

Create a Profile

The profile in the Leadr software we've created includes personal and professional insights about who an employee is and how to work with them. At Leadr, we check these insights before meetings to know how best to work with a co-worker or to see special ways to celebrate someone by providing them with their favorite food, drink, or incentive.

Be in Current Role for 90+ Days

Each role has an adjustment period, so we've taken a 90-day probationary approach before they can start the LeadrU program. However, this isn't a hard and fast rule. If an employee shows a strong desire (and promise) right off the bat, you can implement this as soon as you see fit.

Demonstrates a Desire for Feedback

We believe feedback is the cornerstone of growth. At Leadr, we provide feedback to presenters and peers after every meeting and encourage team members to regularly ask and give feedback to each other. There's no better indicator of a desire for growth than asking for feedback. Especially hard feedback. So we require each employee in our development program to have both given and received feedback in the previous 30 days.

Share Your Current Goals, Projects, and Responsibilities

This is about having the employee communicate, in their own way, what they want to do and where they want to go. It's absolutely critical. There's nothing worse than a manager being prescriptive about where someone else should want to go. If it comes from the top down, it's worthless.

Commitment

Once again, it's about buy-in. We ask each employee to clearly communicate their attention to regular meetings for three months. This is really the minimum, as growth plans should constantly evolve and update.

Schedule a Manager Meeting

Each employee has to schedule a meeting with their manager to discuss their goals and desire to be a part of the program. Once again, a big part of this is about showing initiative. While we're not giving managers an excuse to sit on their hands and not engage their employees, we want to foster a culture where employees can always bring their boss questions, concerns, and ideas.

Employee Sends a Recap

Recaps are essential. We'll talk more about them in the feedback chapter, but we've found that these short memos help avoid issues before they happen, foster clarity, and train people to listen well. After their initial meeting with their manager, every employee is required to send a recap. We want this to become a habit, so we introduce it here.

THE PERSONAL PLAN

Once all the prerequisites are finished, the employee is ready to move on to the second phase, which is a personalized LeadrU plan. Each person's development plan includes several kinds of projects, experiences, and assignments, but it's divided into five key components:

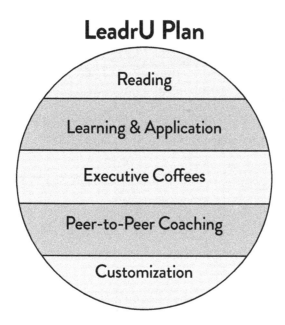

LeadrU Plan

- Reading
- Learning & Application
- Executive Coffees
- Peer-to-Peer Coaching
- Customization

Now, let's explain each aspect.

Reading

At Leadr, we love books and sharing what we've learned from them. Assigning a book helps us combine readings related to our core values while allowing employees to explore areas where they want to develop and pursue their interests. Later in the program, LeadrU participants will complete a project about each of our company's favorite and most influential books, from *The Five Dysfunctions of a Team* to *Radical Candor*. This project helps the team member connect what they've learned from the book to their work at Leadr.

Learning & Applying

LeadrU also includes two monthly learning assignments related to what the team member is reading throughout the program. The assignments help them dig deeper into the topics discussed in the book, challenge and stretch their thinking, and then apply it to their current role at Leadr.

Executive Coffees

Having 1:1 time with executives is a great learning experience. Team members get to hear firsthand from the organization's leaders; we've found that invaluable. This experience offers undivided time for team members to ask questions and request feedback from leaders they likely don't get to speak with on a daily basis. This experience also helps us equip others to step into that role someday, demonstrating the skills and experience they need to strive towards through this program.

Peer-to-Peer Coaching

In addition to conversations with executives, we also know the power of collaborative work with peers. So we host a monthly in-person discussion with others in the LeadrU program, where participants discuss the books they've been reading and how they've changed their perspective. These discussions allow participants to connect their learning to their role at Leadr and their experience on our team.

Conversation starters at these discussions include questions like:

- Tell the team about a time when you broke trust with someone. What damage did it cause? How did you begin rebuilding trust with them?

- Which of the five dysfunctions of a team mentioned in the book do you think you struggle with the most? What's one small step you can take to work on it? How can your team help you?

Stretch Project and Customization

We wrap it all up by creating a personalized growth plan for each individual. Again, what is key about this LeadrU development plan is that it's customizable.

While some sections are required company-wide, there are also sections where the employee's manager can assign projects, reading, or learning that is most relevant to the employee. For example, every employee in LeadrU will read *The Five Dysfunctions of a Team* in the first month and have the opportunity to engage in an exclusive conversation with our CEO. Later in the program, however, there's flexibility in the plan for the employee to focus on and pursue areas of leadership growth they're interested in and passionate about.

It all culminates in what we call a "Stretch Project." The concept here is that the employee chooses an initiative they are interested in that helps them step outside their comfort zone and moves the company forward. Some of our best innovations as a company have come from LeadrU Stretch Projects, including launching our company website in three months and starting our regional thought leadership events we call LeadrTable.

There's nothing more powerful than helping an employee realize they can accomplish more than they ever thought they could and seeing how challenging themselves to grow also grows the company. It's the epitome of the alliance.

***

Those are the central tenets of the program. And here's what it looks like when you put it all together:

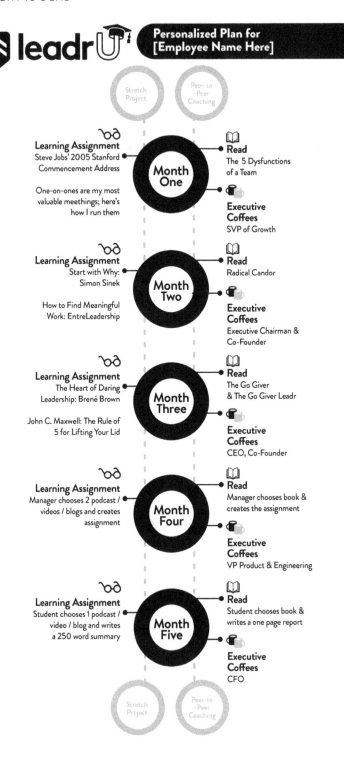

leadrU

Personalized Plan for [Employee Name Here]

Stretch Project

Peer-to-Peer Coaching

Month One

Learning Assignment
Steve Jobs' 2005 Stanford Commencement Address

One-on-ones are my most valuable meethings; here's how I run them

Read
The 5 Dysfunctions of a Team

Executive Coffees
SVP of Growth

Month Two

Learning Assignment
Start with Why: Simon Sinek

How to Find Meaningful Work: EntreLeadership

Read
Radical Candor

Executive Coffees
Executive Chairman & Co-Founder

Month Three

Learning Assignment
The Heart of Daring Leadership: Brené Brown

John C. Maxwell: The Rule of 5 for Lifting Your Lid

Read
The Go Giver & The Go Giver Leadr

Executive Coffees
CEO, Co-Founder

Month Four

Learning Assignment
Manager chooses 2 podcast / videos / blogs and creates assignment

Read
Manager chooses book & creates the assignment

Executive Coffees
VP Product & Engineering

Month Five

Learning Assignment
Student chooses 1 podcast / video / blog and writes a 250 word summary

Read
Student chooses book & writes a one page report

Executive Coffees
CFO

Stretch Project

Peer-to-Peer Coaching

This approach of balancing structure and creativity informed the way we designed LeadrU. A few weeks before the program begins, each participant receives this template to build their customized leadership development plan alongside their manager. For the first three months, nearly all the projects are determined by Leadr, but by month four, as each participant develops, almost every piece of the program is determined by the participant and their manager. This allows employees to act as leaders as they become more independent and confident in their decision-making abilities.

(We've included a sample template in Appendix B to help you understand how this works.)

We want to stress again that how we've structured LeadrU is not how you have to structure your own leadership development program. However, we think it's an excellent way to start, and we want to give you the keys to the car we built. If you want to soup it up or strip it down, that's up to you. However, at minimum, here are the key elements any development program has to have:

- Employee buy-in
- A means to get to know the employee
- Clear goals
- 1-on-1 meetings
- Consistent feedback

Nail those essentials, and you'll have a robust program.

ROLL OUT

There's a reason we put employee buy-in first in the list above. Because without it, nothing happens. You can have the most amazing program in the world, but if the employees aren't bought in – if they don't see the benefit and don't take the initiative – it's all for nothing. But while employee buy-in is key in the entire process, it's not the only buy-in you need to secure.

Before implementing any development program in your organization, get buy-in from those above you as well. If you "go rogue" and put this in place without talking to anyone else, there's a much smaller chance it will actually take root. That doesn't mean you can't implement it for, say, just your team. But if you don't at least get a soft sign-off from other leaders in the organization, the chance of success decreases considerably.

So what happens if you encounter pushback from above? We recommend referencing some of the significant stats we've included in this chapter and others or simply getting them a copy of this book. If it's enough to convince you, hopefully, it will help persuade them as well.

Also, be careful how you roll out the idea of implementing growth plans to those under you. Again, you don't want to be prescriptive. Don't be the parent yelling in the car on the way to the water park, "We're going to have fun whether you like it or not!" Those trips rarely turned out fun.

Instead, begin by asking your employees important questions about themselves, their goals, and how you can do better. Those types of questions are great lead-ins to introducing a robust development program that solves, not creates, problems.

Finally, once you've settled on the program's layout, identified the tools and resources you and the participants will need, and communicated the plan to your organization, it's time to begin developing leaders.

For a smooth program, we recommend planning a few activities and milestones:

- Host an orientation for participants to ask questions and get details before they commit.
- Be sure to track the progress of each participant. We do this through our Leadr people development software.
- Plan a celebration or reception for participants at the end of the program. If you make the program a big deal, your employees will too.

To set you up for success, we've included all the templates mentioned in this chapter in Appendix B at the back, including an email template to help you roll it out. In the end, we want to prepare you and equip you for success. We've found that the most successful leadership programs get buy-in from people on multiple levels and are rolled out after healthy conversations among key stakeholders occur.

So here's to your growth and development, and the growth and development of those under and around you.

CHAPTER 5
SETTING CLEAR GOALS

CHRIS

The situation was dire. More so than we could initially let on to the entire company.

We were in the middle of a big capital raise at Pushpay, and our sales numbers were not good. And do you know what's an absolute business killer? Plummeting sales numbers in the middle of a capital raise. We needed to turn things around and quickly. So we decided to implement some pretty drastic and clear goals.

That's where Amanda comes in. More on her in a bit, though.

First, we had an apparent problem. If we didn't hit our sales goal, we would run out of money and tank our capital raise. That meant there would likely be no Pushpay after the quarter if things didn't turn around. The pressure was on.

Matt and I have an agreement and plan for these types of situations. When you're behind, like we were, there are two things you dial up: the work ethic and the communication. In other words, we work hard, get creative, and constantly talk about it.

We say things like: "Here's what I'm trying. Here's what's working. Here's what's not working."

The idea is, if we lose, we're not going to lose because we didn't work hard enough or because there was a communication breakdown.

So this particular quarter, I came to Matt and laid it all out there. We needed to show even more growth for the potential investors, so I gave him an aggressive goal. I told him we needed to hit the numbers—no ifs, ands, or buts. The situation was that dire. I made the goal clear and the consequences of not reaching that goal even clearer. Not in a threatening way, but in a truthful way. No numbers, no business.

MATT

I remember that conversation well. It wasn't a fun one, but it was eye-opening. And there was no way around it. I took what Chris told me and then had a conversation with the sales team. That's a clear distinction, by the way. I had a conversation with them. I invited them into the problem. I didn't yell at them, I didn't intimidate them, and I didn't threaten them. I talked with them.

To start, I put together a presentation. And in fact, I called an audible. We'll get into this more in Chapter 7, but I decided I needed to be even more vulnerable with my team than I was initially comfortable with. I needed them to understand precisely what the problem was and invite them into the solution.

So I told them, "Hey everyone, we're in a pickle. Our numbers are down, and it could spell some really bad things if we don't hit our goal." In fact, in the Powerpoint presentation, I included a picture of an ambulance and emergency room on the final slide. The idea was clear: We'd be on life support if we didn't hit the goal.

I then offered up a solution and asked them what they thought. That's also important. As a manager, your job isn't to point out problems and wait for answers to come to you. (But that's what a lot of managers do.) You need to offer solutions. Even if they're bad ones, it's better to give people a starting point and invite them to poke holes in it so they can help you develop something better.

So what was my solution?

"I'd really like you all to come in at six in the morning," I told the sales team. "It's optional, but we sure would appreciate it if you could give us a little extra so we can achieve this important goal. Because we might not have a company in two months if we miss it."

I didn't stop there.

"It's obvious what happens if we don't hit this," I said. "But if we do hit it, we're going to fly everyone to Disneyland."

Yes, Disneyland.

We had a Pushpay summit planned for the next quarter, where we would fly in our top clients and prospective clients. And while the guest list initially included only certain people at the company, we decided that if we hit this goal, we would extend it to everyone.

I wish I could tell you everyone responded ecstatically. That people were there around the clock every day. But that's not the case. Who did "get it"?

Amanda.

CHRIS

The next morning, I showed up to the office at 6 a.m. I didn't think we could ask people to give up a couple of extra hours if I wasn't willing to do the same. When I walked in, I was shocked at what I saw: one of our least experienced sales teams making cold calls with smiles on their faces.

And who was leading them? Amanda.

Do you know how old Amanda was at the time? She was 23. I only mention that to point out she wasn't some seasoned sales lead with years of experience. But what she lacked in experience, she made up for in work ethic.

"Hey Chris, good morning," she said cheerily, but also with a hint of matter-of-factness.

I returned the greeting and walked to my office in disbelief. Not because I didn't think anyone would take Matt up on his offer, but because of who took him up on it. As I got set up, I noticed Amanda making coffee for everyone. She had a personal Nespresso machine on her desk, and I don't think I've ever seen a coffee maker work that hard. The moment one cup was done, she took orders and made another. She wasn't only a team lead; she was a barista.

As soon as I saw that, I knew what I had to do. I left the office and went to the nearest store. When I returned, I plopped a box of 50 Nespresso pods on her desk. "This is the least I can do," I told her. Her face lit up. She told me later that little gesture made her feel seen.

So did Amanda and her team immediately put us over the top? Nope. Initially, it didn't even move the needle. In fact, the numbers weren't going in the right direction even two weeks into extra shifts and extra work.

But we knew the goal, and we stuck with it. Amanda did, too. And in the second half of the month, things completely turned around. Eventually, we hit the goal. We got the investment. And when we did, people went berserk. I've never seen anything like it before in my life. People were chanting, cheering, and clapping, losing their minds all across the office.

And you know what? We all went to Disney.

GOOD GOAL REMINDERS

So what's the point of all that? Amanda's story demonstrates some valuable, foundational aspects that apply to all types of goals:

1. Goals must be clear to be effective.
2. Goals should have both carrots and sticks.
3. Empower people to reach those goals.
4. While people like to achieve goals, people work for people.

Let's tackle the first bullet point. I gave Matt a very clear goal, and Matt gave his team a very clear goal. He laid out both the consequences of missing that goal and the benefits of achieving it. Amanda, in turn, rallied around that goal and then broke it down for her team.[41] There was no ambiguity. There was no insinuation. There was no guessing. That's important when it comes to goals. Too often, we're scared to actually set the goal we want to achieve. Maybe we think it's too lofty. Maybe we're afraid people will be overwhelmed. Maybe we don't want to appear pushy. Whatever it is, we tend to shroud our goals instead of stating them clearly, both as companies and as individuals.

But here's the thing: I would take a clear goal that's too ambitious any day

---

41 We weren't asking her team alone to meet the goal for the entire sales team, by the way. What we were asking was for her to rally around the goal and then synthesize it for her direct reports.

over a murky, more achievable goal. Why? It doesn't mean I'm against more achievable goals, which we'll discuss in a minute. But it's because clear goals actually inspire people more than you think. And I've also found that failing to reach a clear goal offers a lot of clarity. Sometimes it can reveal bad leadership, bad personnel, or even bad processes. And that's a good thing!

So what do clear goals look like? Let's use another football analogy.

A head coach can try and inspire his team by saying, "Our goal is to score more points than the other team." He's not wrong. But that's everyone's goal! If you want to win a game, any game, your goal is to score more points. But a lot of people have lost football games rallying around the goal of scoring more points than the opponent.

Instead, some of the best coaches break down bigger goals into smaller ones that are clearer. Maybe it's, "We're going to win the turnover ratio," or, "We're going to win the rushing battle." Those are still "big" goals, but they're a lot more realistic; they're a lot more clear. And I hope you can see that, even though they're big, because they're clearer, they become more attainable. And statistics show, for example, that a team that wins the turnover battle is much more likely to win the football game and reach the ultimate goal of "scoring more points."

Edwin Locke, the 1960s pioneer in goal-setting theory, found that "a clear, measurable goal is more achievable than one that is poorly defined."[42] In other words, it's no coincidence that clearer goals tend to be more achievable. That's why setting clear goals matters.

Several psychological reasons support Locke's analysis. Most importantly, when

---

42 Edwin Locke, "Toward a Theory or Task Motivation and Incentives." Organizational Behavior and Human Performance 3, no. 2 (May 1968): 157-189. https://doi.org/10.1016/0030-5073(68)90004-4.

we clearly identify what we want, the brain receives a signal that puts it on high alert to pay more attention to opportunities, patterns, and pitfalls. This hyper-focus points the brain in a specific direction, allowing it to draw more connections and think more effectively. In his book, *Measure What Matters*, investor and author John Doerr describes action-oriented goals as a "vaccine against fuzzy thinking."[43] Those who know exactly what they are working on excel at productivity, achieving what they want in a shorter time frame.

It's critical, then, that companies achieve clarity at an executive level first. Goals should be so specifically defined that there is no room for varying interpretations. Each team and individual must be able to articulate how their work directly impacts the company's success. As one Harvard Business Review survey makes clear, simply communicating your company's goals to the organization does not automatically equal understanding.[44] In fact, the 2019 Achievers employee engagement survey found that only 4 in 10 employees know their company's vision, and 57% are unmotivated by the guiding mission.[45] There has to be ownership, and ownership starts with clarity.

I'll say this about the second bullet point: Carrots and sticks are crucial. There has to be a push and a pull. A word of caution, though: Don't fall into the trap of making the "stick" all about someone losing their job. That's not motivating.

"But Chris, Matt made it clear to the team that not achieving the goal could very well mean the end of their jobs!"

You're right. He did. But he did so after much thought and, frankly,

43 John Doerr, Measure What Matters: How Google, Bono, and The Gates Foundation Rock the World with OKRs (New York: Portfolio/Penguin, 2018, Kindle Edition), 7.

44 Donald Sull, Rebecca Homkes, Charles Sull, "Why Strategy Execution Unravels - and What to Do About It." Harvard Business Review, March 2015. https://hbr.org/2015/03/why-strategy-execution-unravelsand-what-to-do-about-it

45 "The Complacency Effect: Despite Disengagement, Employees Plan to Stay at Their Jobs." Achievers, March 2019. https://www.achievers.com/resources/white-papers/achievers-complacency-report/

consternation. It was the final card he had to play because it accurately reflected reality. And that's why it worked.

If you make the "stick" of every goal that someone's job is on the line if they don't hit it, it won't be long before they call your bluff. It worked in this instance because it was the truth. But I've seen too many company leaders try to "motivate" their people by threatening their jobs, creating a culture of fear and distrust. As a result, it leads to higher turnover, more burnout, and low morale. When you're defining your sticks, base them on reality, not drama. You'll experience significant benefits if you do.

Regarding the third bullet point, as a people developer, how you empower your people to reach their goals matters, too. I'm not claiming to have done anything heroic by buying Amanda a pack of Nespresso pods, but that simple act went much further than I realized in the moment. She said she felt seen. And do you know what employees who feel seen do? They go above and beyond. More often than not, they hit their goals. They hit your company's goals.

We talked earlier in the book about creating a framework, a playbook, for your team to be successful. One of those "plays" is doing whatever it takes for your team to feel seen, heard, and empowered. That may look like an extra work-from-home day, a new project management software, or it may look like a pack of 50 Nespresso pods. Whatever it is, the point is clear: Empower your people.

Finally, and this goes hand-in-hand with the previous point, it's not just the goal and the reward that inspires people. It's people who inspire people. When I plopped those pods on Amanda's desk, I put a face to the goal. At that moment, she wasn't just trying to hit numbers, avoid a layoff, or even go to Disney. She was working for me because I was working with her. I became, in a sense, the physical manifestation of the goal. I can't overstate how important that is.

So as you work with your people to create and convey goals, remember that people prefer working for and with people toward a clear goal. That's more motivating than you realize.

CHRIS AND MATT

TYPES OF GOALS

Now that we've established the important aspects of goal-setting, it's important to talk about the numerous types of goals that you can set. These are the ones we encounter most often in our business, so we want to tackle some of the prevailing theories and differences between them.

Personal Goals

We put this chapter here because it's the natural next step after adopting a personalized growth plan. That's important because every personalized growth plan and leadership development program must include setting clear, personal goals.

Personal goals are aspirations to strengthen a character trait or change a lifestyle habit. These goals often center on fitness, family, education, finances, or career. In our context, as a people developer, you must encourage employees to set personal goals that stretch their professional vision, such as earning an industry certification, increasing job performance metrics, or improving time management skills.

This is where personal growth plans come in. When an employee starts going through your leadership development program, they must set personal goals (as we outlined in the last chapter). In fact, before you ever ask an employee to partake in a company goal, you have to get them to set a personal goal. Why? Because it all comes back to buy-in. As a people developer, your job is to ensure your employee sees how helping the company attain a goal works for their personal benefit. That's the new landscape we're in. Employees must see how helping meet a sales goal, for example, plays into their personal goal of eventually becoming a team lead.

That's exactly what happened with Amanda. She had a personal goal of growing her team-building skills. As a young employee, she saw how that could get her to a higher leadership position. So when we presented her with the important team goal, it became much more inspiring for her to tackle because she saw how it fit into her personal goal of developing her leadership skills. And she absolutely crushed it.

Personal development goals, then, support team goals. When each person has the opportunity to shine using their skill set and the freedom to innovate, they find a deeper meaning in their work. As we've shown you, that sense of ownership fosters engagement and passion for doing better. And when individual goals challenge employees to stretch their professional skills, it ultimately benefits the team and organization as a whole.

Company and Team Goals

As a manager, you're not only responsible for helping shape and approve your employees' personal goals, but you'll also be responsible for creating and conveying company and team goals in some way.

When it comes to company goals, they should focus on a handful of initiatives that can make a real difference. These are centered on the why and tie back to the organization's mission and values. While focused and clear, they are also broad enough to apply to every level of the business. Doerr explains that conviction and buy-in start at the top, and he quotes Intuit CEO Bill Campbell to do it: "If you don't model it, no one's going to do it."[46]

"An effective goal-setting system starts with disciplined thinking at the top,

---

46 Doerr, *Measure What Matters*, 49.

with leaders who invest the time and energy to choose what counts," he adds.[47]

Team goals, as opposed to company goals, tend to be project-based or metric-driven, such as hitting a sales target to drive growth. By leveraging each member's diverse strengths, team goals can propel the company further. This approach also promotes real collaboration and teamwork, which builds trust, unity, and pride in the outcome. Successful teams encourage collaboration and provide space for new ideas, but they also hold each other accountable to company and team goals.

Annual to Daily Goals

Annual goals represent the long-term vision you want to accomplish. These big-picture targets support the company mission and serve as a blueprint for prioritizing an action plan. This broader scope takes more time, so you need to break it down into smaller action steps that you can do right now to achieve the bigger dream.

Organizing goals into quarterly, monthly, weekly, and daily tasks makes reaching the end goal more manageable and keeps you grounded in the present instead of daydreaming about your ambitions. Meeting those minor milestones establishes accountability and motivates you to power on by giving you "easy" wins.

Goals vs. Tasks

Goals are like mile markers on a map, pointing us toward the work that needs to be done to fulfill our why. Each goal is specific in identifying the desired outcome, how success will be measured, relevancy to the mission, and when it will be completed. Goals are limited in number. The sweet spot appears to be between three and five to maintain focus.

Tasks, however, are the many action steps we take to achieve those goals. Don't

47 Doerr, Measure What Matters, 47.

confuse tasks with goals. Organizing these smaller "hows" into daily lists keeps you moving forward and helps you manage your time more efficiently. Progress on tasks proves that you are moving closer to achieving your goals. Items that make it onto your list that do not relate to the overall mission should be delegated or nixed from your to-do list. More on that below.

Strategic Goals

Companies cannot operate efficiently without a unifying target. When everyone is aligned with the company's core principles, they can work together toward the same goal. Alignment on a single objective creates shared cultural values, nurtures trust in leadership, and motivates everyone to put in their best, coordinated effort.

That starts with defining your "why." In his Ted Talk, "Why the Secret to Success is Setting the Right Goal," Doerr explains that hitting objectives and numbers is not enough to achieve real growth. Instead, the "why" has to come first and inform individual objectives.[48]

Still, Harvard Business Review (HBR) data shows that managers consistently rely too much on "translating strategy into objectives, cascading those objectives down the hierarchy, measuring progress, and rewarding performance." Why? Because it allows them to place failure on the shoulders of a "breakdown in the processes" and wipe their hands clean.[49]

The problem with this approach is that it fails to engage the entire team in the goal-setting process, which diminishes buy-in. The HBR study found that only half of managers understand how their priorities fit with the company's major initiatives. That number drops to 30% among those reporting to senior

---

48 John Doerr, "Why the Secret to Success is Setting the Right Goals." TED 2018. Lecture presented at The Age of Amazement, 2023.

49 Sull, Homkes, and Sull, "Why Strategy Execution Unravels" (no. 5)

executives and a mere 16% of frontline employees.

Alignment isn't about handing down directives that everyone must follow. Instead, each person must understand "why" and participate in the decision-making process. Consistent commitment to the goals happens when they have the freedom to determine which of their own contributions will best support the progress toward the core objectives. Strategic goals should still be set at the executive level and then cascade down, but only as a guide for establishing the team and individual goals. All goals should also ladder up, connecting directly to the level above and below to create overall alignment with everyone working toward one set of goals.

Permission to say "No"

Warren Buffet once said that "the difference between successful people and really successful people is that really successful people say no to almost everything."[50] That means you need to give your people the power to say "no." That may seem counterintuitive, but let us explain.

Inherent in establishing clear goals is the ability to make informed decisions about direction and prioritization. It's much easier to say "no" to activities and extra tasks when you have a great reason. When you are clear about your goals, both with yourself and with others, you are hyper-aware of which actions distract and which actions propel you forward. Attending an unnecessary meeting, working on a superfluous task, or constantly chasing new ideas gobbles up the precious time you should spend on higher-value projects.

That's what we mean by empowering your people to say "no." And yet we find ourselves in a time when people think that they're failing if they're not overwhelmed – if they're not constantly "hustling."

---

50 Marcel Schwantes, "Warren Buffet Says What Separates Successful People From Everyone Else Really Comes Down to a Two-Letter Word." Inc.com, November 2021. https://www.inc.com/marcel-schwantes/warren-buffett-says-what-separates-successful-people-from-everyone-else-really-comes-down-to-a-2-letter-word.html

Michael Hyatt, an author and former publishing company CEO, warns about the dangers of the hustle fallacy in his book Free to Focus. Fear of missing a game-changing opportunity or disappointing others drives us to say "yes" to too many opportunities. However, that creates an environment where we are constantly working on a never-ending list of tasks instead of actually moving the company forward. Rather than getting closer to achieving our goals, we are left feeling overwhelmed and too exhausted to do anything extra.

"The hard work comes in summoning the courage to say no to requests that aren't important and to eliminate those unimportant tasks that are already eating up your time and energy," Hyatt explains.[51]

If you set a clear goal or goals, your people can't feel handcuffed or bogged down – they have to feel empowered. So empower them with the ability to say "no!" It does wonders for productivity.

Measuring Success

Being clear about not only your goals but also what success looks like is critical to proving that you have achieved your goals. Clear success metrics leave no question that you (or your employees) have reached or fallen short of the destination. It is not enough to write down your goals and action steps in a way that they can be quantified. To really level up, you have to share your plans and progress with others. You have to seek accountability.

One study conducted by psychology professor Dr. Gail Matthews, proved that incorporating accountability is crucial to the success of a goal. In the control group, participants were asked to only think about their goals. Only 4 in 10 people achieved success. In contrast, the group that shared weekly progress

---

51 Michael Hyatt, Free to Focus: A Total Productivity System to Achieve More by Doing Less (Grand Rapids, Michigan: Baker, 2019, Kindle Edition), 92.

updates with a specific person had a whopping 76% success rate.[52]

Plans fall through – goals die – without practical measurement. So check in on a regular basis to monitor progress, review feedback, and make adjustments as needed. As Doerr notes, "An effective goal management system respects targets and deadlines while adapting to circumstances."[53]

"Contributors are most engaged when they can actually see how their work contributes to the company's success," Doerr writes. "Quarter to quarter, day to day, they look for tangible measures of their achievement. Extrinsic rewards – the year-end bonus check – merely validate what they already know."[54]

We've pursued clarity in this aspect by always ensuring each goal has a clear owner. There's an old saying that if you ask two people to feed your dog, the dog will die. Why? Because no one actually owns the objective. Similarly, if you have two people responsible for a goal, that goal will die.

Can different departments share a goal? Absolutely. However, there still needs to be a clear owner. Different departments can own smaller sub-goals or tasks, but there has to be a specific owner of the overall goal.

There's something interesting that happens when you take that approach. The goal, not you, ends up managing the team or the people. What we mean is that, if a goal is clear and properly owned, a manager shouldn't have to constantly seek updates on the tasks and objectives needed to meet it. When people own a goal, they self-report. And that's a beautiful thing because it frees you up.[55]

---

52 Marla Tabaka, "New Study Says This Simple Step Will Increase the Odds of Achievhing Your Goals (Substantially)." Inc. com, January 2019. https://www.inc.com/marla-tabaka/this-study-found-1-simple-step-to-practically-guarantee-youll-achieve-your-goals-for-real.html

53 Doerr, Measure What Matters, 10.

54 Doerr, Measure What Matters, 114.

55 We've included more details on different goal-setting methods in Appendix C.

Common Mistakes

So what are some of the common mistakes we see in goal setting? The main one is an overemphasis on task performance. While tasks are important, and breaking down goals into smaller objectives is similarly so, you'll create many problems for yourself and within your organization, if you measure success solely based on checking off to-dos.

We explain that more below, where we've created a checklist to help ensure that you don't fall into some of the common issues that derail the goal process and lead to poor results:

- **Top-Level Cascading Decisions.** Setting goals for others that are only decided from the top and then cascade down to every level has numerous problems. First, it creates a loss of agility as everyone waits for the trickle-down changes. The greatest challenge to executing strategy is a manager's inability to seize opportunities, mitigate emerging threats, or react quickly. Even worse, innovation sits trapped at the outside edges of the organization when frontline employees are marginalized in the goal-setting process.

- **Irrelevant Goals.** Goals that do not push you toward your greater purpose are just distractions. Organizations will never nurture engagement or achieve meaningful growth if their strategies conflict with their identity and core values. Goals that are set by those who are detached from the work required to accomplish the goal will also feel irrelevant to the employee. Other reasons goals become outdated include lack of frequent updating and inflexibility to changing circumstances. This creates fragmentation in focus and alignment on the most important priorities.

- **Vague and Hidden Plans.** Goals that are too general do not inspire. Others may create excitement without direction, measurability, or accountability. Doerr warns against the dangers of getting people whipped up with enthusiasm but not providing direction on what to do with it. Goals are not standalone adjectives, such as becoming richer, healthier, or less stressed. You will quickly give up if you are not specific about how much money you want or what "happy" looks like to you. Private goals that are not written down or obscured in silos create non-collaborative teams that fail to align.

- **Fragmented Focus.** Having more than five active goals splits your focus on what is most important. Laundry list goals are also harder to circulate and coordinate with other teams. Often, a laundry list of goals means you have compiled a task list instead of a challenging set of goals that require growth.

- **Too Big, Too Soon.** While you should stretch yourself, the goal must be achievable. Excellent goals fail by not allowing sufficient time, assigning massive benchmarks, or being tied to factors beyond your control. Plans also flop when you fail to think through potential obstacles and ways to obtain resources you don't currently have but will need.

- **Focusing Only on KPIs.** KPIs (key performance indicators) provide important data on the "what," but when used alone, they do not shine a light on the "how" or "why." Performance-based goals do not provide clear direction or recognize milestones, so managers miss valuable opportunities to teach and encourage ownership.

One final note here: A performance-driven culture focused on tasks is also a terrible metric for determining bonuses and salaries. The fair question in these circumstances is, "If risk is penalized, then why chance it?" The HBR study we mentioned earlier revealed that two-thirds of managers would advise new colleagues to make commitments that they know are attainable rather than stretching for ambitious goals. When the definition of failure is based on task completion, growth will become stagnant.

And that leads us to the next section.

CHRIS

STRETCHING YOURSELF

As we begin closing out this chapter, there's one other thing I want to make clear about goals that expands on the idea of task-based management and the stagnancy it produces. Goals, especially personal goals, have to stretch the employee – they have to stretch you.[56] You can't just pad a personal development plan, for example, with softballs. Of course, as we mentioned above, they can't be outrageous. They still have to be attainable.

That brings me to Jason.

Jason was one of our sales leads at Pushpay and was one of our top performers. One day he came to us and said he was going to start looking for another job. When we asked him why, he said he felt he had learned all he could at Pushpay about sales.

On the one hand, that's certainly possible. As we mentioned earlier in the book, you will have top performers that outgrow their role, and if you don't have a position to promote them into, you should support them on their way out.

But in this instance, we didn't quite agree with Jason. We felt there was more he could learn. So we pressed him a bit. I asked him, "What are some things you need to improve on to go from where you are currently to the sales role you want to have?"

---

56 That's also why we included the "stretch project" when it comes to personal development plans mentioned in Chapter 4.

His answer? "Well, I probably need to get better at public speaking." Without even flinching, I said, "Great! You just signed up to speak at our next all-hands meeting in front of 350 people."

He was shocked. But I was dead serious. Why? Because when it comes to goals, it's absolutely necessary to stretch yourself. It was obvious that Jason had become a little stagnant. By his own admission, he wasn't growing. That led him to believe he had learned everything he could learn with us. But in reality, by asking him what he needed to improve on, he revealed an area of personal growth and that, in fact, he hadn't learned everything he needed to propel him into his next role, job, or company. So as a people developer, I wanted to give him the immediate opportunity to grow.

That stretched Jason, but it also stretched me. Why? Because while he had to take a risk in getting up in front of 350 people, I also had to take the risk of putting him up in front of those people and the very real possibility that he could fail. You, as a manager, have to be willing to do that. You have to be willing to give people the room to try, to stretch, to grow, and even to fail.

It just so happens that, in this case, once Jason got up there, he absolutely crushed it. I wasn't positive that would happen, but I was willing to take the risk. And we, as a company, and Jason, as a person, were better for it.

This same concept is prevalent in sports and personal training. (Are you starting to sense a theme here?) If you really want to grow as an athlete, it's critical to take on more than you're comfortable with. Any athletic coach worth their salt will start by asking their athlete or athletes where they want to go and then help them develop a plan that stretches them.

Consider this example:

"Do you want to be an Olympic swimmer?"

"Yes."

"Great. I'll see you tomorrow at 5:00 AM."

Why? Because you can't just magically flip a switch and be an Olympic swimmer. You have to get uncomfortable in your training. You have to put in the grueling early-morning hours in the pool. You have to be sore. You have to make yourself uncomfortable.

We tell employees a lot that they have to be six months ahead of the growth of the business. Or said another way, they have to actually be training for the job they want, not the one they have. Why? So when they do finally get the opportunity (either with our company or elsewhere), the company and the team aren't waiting for them to grow.

That's exactly what I did in the run-up to making Matt VP of sales. Asking him for his sales plan was only the final step in getting him ready, even though he didn't know it. So when I finally elevated him to that role, he was ready. He had done the growing, the stretching, and the training.

That's the idea you have to impart to your employees. You have to get them so used to stretching themselves so that when they do get promoted, they're ready to do the required work. They've learned the skills and developed the important habits. Otherwise, it's too late.

What does that look like practically? I always tell people, "Dress for the job you want, invite yourself to meetings you don't need to be in, learn about how different departments work, and create big goals for yourself."

If you want to be an Olympic swimmer, you can't skip your training, show up on the race day, and expect to keep up. It's impossible. It's the same concept in business and with professional growth. In the military, they say that you default to your training in the heat of battle. That's why they train so much!

So if you want that big promotion, that fancy title, that pay raise even, it's incumbent upon you to stretch yourself. Make goals that are small enough to accomplish but big enough to require you – or your employee – to level up to achieve them. "When you're committed to a goal, looking ahead at how far you have left to go is motivating. Staring at the summit fuels grit," author and leadership expert Adam Grant writes.[57] "When doubt creeps in, you're better off looking back at how far you've already come. Seeing your progress builds confidence and commitment."

That's the mentality of Olympic swimmers. It needs to be your mentality, too.

CHRIS AND MATT

FINAL THOUGHTS

We've covered a lot in this chapter, and that's because goals are absolutely critical to your success, the success of your employees, and the success of your company. So we wanted to summarize the keys to effective goal setting:

- Effective goals are clear.
- Effective goals stretch yourself and your employees.
- Effective goals are collaborative throughout the defining, maintaining, revising, and reporting processes. Ideally, this collaboration is cross-discipline, and the final product inspires and furthers your mission.
- Effective goals are set using a mix of both top-down and self-imposed

---

57 Adam Grant. "When you're committed to a goal, it's motivating to look ahead at how far you have left to go." Facebook, October 14, 2022. https://www.facebook.com/photo/?fbid=670874041067123&set= pb.100044335993931.-2207520000.

objectives to fully involve the entire organization in planning and decision-making. This strategy nurtures a culture of ownership and achievement.

- Effective goals, and your progress toward those goals, are transparent across your peers, other teams, and the organization. To build trust, open communication about challenges, successes, and industry changes must flow both ways.
- Effective goals are regularly revisited and adjusted as needed to ensure they are the most relevant top priorities at all times.
- Effective goals utilize a management system that assigns tasks, tracks progress, and sends automatic reminders to update goals.

How do we know this works? Well, one of the reasons is that Amanda – who we started this chapter talking about – eventually ended up leaving Pushpay.

We know that sounds silly, but it's true. See, Amanda is the perfect example of how clear personal and company-wide goals lead to incredible results. After she stepped up, throughout the next year, Amanda stretched herself. She grew. She became an absolute rockstar.

So when she came to us and told us she was leaving, we had all the confidence in the world that she had leveled up in and was prepared for more. She became an HR executive at a massive e-commerce platform in Europe.

Why? Because she embraced goals. She realized that, to get where she wanted to go, goals were essential to her development. And as she embraced those goals, we benefited. Did she embrace our company goals because she was a lifer? No. She embraced them because she saw how they paved her path for future growth.

That's the kind of culture you need to create. You will lose some great people. But you will also retain a lot more. And your organization will be better for it.

CHAPTER 6
1-ON-1 MEETINGS

MATT

I thought for sure I was getting fired.

I was a young sales leader working my way up at Pushpay. But despite climbing the ladder, something vital was missing: regular communication with my boss.

So when my manager, Alex, scheduled a lunch meeting with me, I was scared. I even texted my wife, "Hey, just a heads up. I think this is it." That's because Alex had never so much as asked me how my weekend was, let alone asked me out to lunch. He never showed me he cared.

"This is the weirdest thing ever," I remember thinking.

So I showed up to the lunch, albeit reluctantly and skittish, especially considering it was at a Whole Foods, a location that took the least amount of thought imaginable. And you know what happened? It was one of the most awkward moments of my life. That's not an exaggeration.

Alex proceeded to ask me very surface-level questions like someone had a knife to his back and was forcing him to talk. I would answer him, expecting things to get better. But they never actually got better. It was like the world's worst speed dating exercise. It felt like an act, probably because it was. And when I asked him questions, hoping he would open up a little, he gave me nothing. Zero. Zilch.

When we returned to the office, I was so confused: "What just happened?"

I sought Chris out to get some clarity.

"Hey, something really odd just happened," I explained. "Alex took me out to lunch, and it was one of the worst, most forced conversations I've ever had. Is something going on? Do I need to be worried?"

CHRIS

I knew Alex was failing at leadership.

Sure, he was focused on his day-to-day tasks, but it was at the expense of the relationships he was supposed to be fostering. He never showed genuine interest in his team outside of what they could do for them. He was regularly a jerk to his employees, and I could see he was losing them – especially Matt.

So I told Alex he needed to invest in his team. He needed to get to know them, to understand them. His bright idea of how to do that? Taking Matt to Whole Foods for a forced lunch.

As soon as Matt told me what had happened, I shook my head. Alex had completely missed the point. It wasn't about manufacturing care and conversation. It was about demonstrating genuine interest. It wasn't about checking a box. It was about learning. And it was about doing that regularly in a 1-on-1 setting that fostered trust, not some forced one-off.

Did Alex technically fulfill my request? I guess. But he failed the overall assignment. And he failed big time.

MATT

That story perfectly sums up the importance of properly-conducted 1-on-1 meetings, the topic we're covering in this chapter.

In fact, that experience with Alex – as awful as it was – became an inspiration for how I would not do things when I became VP of sales. Put simply, I never wanted anyone under me to experience what I did with him.

Remember the Bob story from the introduction? He was the set-in-his-ways sales VP who had difficulty connecting with his team. He is who I replaced after Chris asked me to put together an impromptu sales plan.

As I mentioned in the introduction, the first thing I did when I got the role was to get to know the team members. How did I do that? I conducted 1-on-1 meetings. I conducted forty 1-on-1 meetings. Not just a couple. Not just a few. Forty.

While it wasn't easy, something incredible happened.

Sitting down with people and asking how they were really doing, addressing any elephants in the room, and offering to help almost immediately began to rebuild some of that lost trust. Slowly but surely, the culture turned around. We flipped management on its head from "top-down" to "bottom-up." By listening to their issues and making changes in response, the team truly started to feel like leadership was there to support them and equip them to be better, as opposed to just being beaten over the head with a stick. Within 60 days, our team broke the record for the most sales in company history. And the following month? We beat that record again.

That quarter became the perfect case study for how people development is more effective than plain, old-fashioned people management.

Here's the thing, though. While those meetings went a long way toward turning around the culture and building trust, I started getting some hard feedback a few months later. While I started strong with 1-on-1 meetings, I took for granted how important they were after the crisis was over. In fact, I regularly started canceling them because I thought the team was "good."

They weren't. Or at least not how I thought they were. See, they needed those 1-on-1 meetings to stay good, not just to get good. And if I didn't continue to take them seriously, I would end up exactly like Bob.

That's one of the main lessons of this chapter. In so many ways, 1-on-1 meetings are how you put everything we've talked about into practice up to this point. They're how you forge an alliance with your people. They're how you develop and implement personalized growth plans. They're how you create and follow up on clear goals. And as we'll see in the next chapter, they are the foundation for giving and receiving effective feedback.

You can't afford to take them for granted.

CHRIS AND MATT

WHY 1-ON-1 MEETINGS ARE IMPORTANT

The benefits of regular, effective 1-on-1 meetings are especially important when considering the new workforce we've been discussing. As we've mentioned, this new workforce wants to feel involved, invested in, and invaluable.

"Today's job market is highly dynamic and transparent," writes Deloitte's Nathan Sloan. "High-potential young employees want regular feedback and career progression advice, not just 'once and done' reviews."[58]

The "regular feedback" Sloan is talking about is accomplished via the 1-on-1 meeting.

Maybe the idea of 1-on-1 meetings seems a little too "touchy-feely," and that makes you hesitant. First, we'll start by saying no one is suggesting that 1-on-1 meetings must be painfully sappy. They just have to be filled with genuine care.

But let's say for the sake of argument that maybe, just maybe, you as a people developer are forced to be a little more open, a little more honest, and a little more "touchy-feely." The research says that the benefits are astronomical if you're willing to do that.

One study from MetrixGlobal LLC showed a 529% ROI from regular 1-on-1 meetings. There's an important caveat, though. Those meetings have to involve some form of coaching. That shouldn't surprise you by now because coaching is a staple of the alliance we've talked about. From the executive summary of the study, "The bottom line: Coaching produced a 529% ROI (that's $5 for every $1 spent on coaching) as well as significant intangible benefits to the business."[59]

Any executive or leader worth their salt can see the benefit in those numbers. In other words, the numbers show it's worth it if you're willing to get real and vulnerable, offer coaching and feedback, and get to know your people by meeting with them consistently. Even if it might be a little uncomfortable at first.

---

58 Nathan Sloan, "Performance Management." Deloitte, February 2015, https://www2.deloitte.com/us/en/insights/focus/human-capital-trends/2015/performance-management-redesign-human-capital-trends-2015.html

59 Merrill Anderson, "Executive Briefing: Case Study on the Return on Investment of Executive Coaching." MetrixGlobal, 2002. https://researchportal.coachingfederation.org/Document/Pdf/abstract_681

But while those numbers speak volumes, we also want to offer practical proof. That leads us to the "Sunday Scaries."

The Sunday Scaries

In the end, your number one job as a people developer is to provide clarity to your employees about where they stand. That's how you become a good leader. It's how you grow, how they grow, and how your company grows.

That's where the "Sunday Scaries" come in.

Maybe you've heard this term; maybe you haven't. In short, it's the weekly anxiety that so many employees get as they start thinking about returning to the work week as their weekend winds down. It sets in around 4 pm on Sundays (3:58 pm to be exact), as people start going over everything they're getting ready to tackle at work.[60]

And according to a LinkedIn study, it's rampant, as "80% of professionals experience the Sunday Scaries, with over 90% of Millennials and Generation Z reporting they feel it."[61]

Those are staggering numbers. And it gives us an opportunity to remind you that Millennials and Gen Z now make up the majority of the workforce.

"This feeling, whether we call it anxiety, worry, stress, fear, whatever, it's all really the same thing," Jonathan Abramowitz, a clinical psychologist and professor at the University of North Carolina at Chapel Hill, tells The Atlantic.

---

60 "Study: Majority of Americans Come Down With a Case of the 'Sunday Scaries' Every Week." SWNS, January 2020. https://swns-research.medium.com/study-majority-of-americans-come-down-with-a-case-of-the-sunday-scaries-every-week-2ce405acb626

61 Blair Heitmann, "Your Guide to Winning @Work: Decoding the Sunday Scaries." LinkedIn, September 2018. https://blog.linkedin.com/2018/september/28/your-guide-to-winning-work-decoding-the-sunday-scaries

"Psychologically, it's a response to the perception of some sort of threat."[62]

In other words, at minimum, 80% of your employees struggle every week with coming to work. After all, they're scared because they perceive a threat. Maybe it's that they don't feel adequate, maybe it's that they don't feel equipped, or maybe it's that they have a deadline they're not sure they're going to hit. Or maybe, they don't have a boss who regularly talks with them – who invests in them.

That latter point we have found forms the basis of so many "scaries." And that means one of the best ways to combat them – to prevent and treat the epidemic of the Sunday Scaries in your office – is to conduct regular 1-on-1 meetings. Why? Because at the heart of why so many people are scared and feel threatened is a lack of clarity. They don't know they're actually doing a good job. They don't know they can ask their manager to equip them better. They don't know that the deadline mentioned in passing is a soft one and not a hard one. They don't know that their boss actually cares about them.

In fact, too many employees show up every Monday wondering if they're getting fired or promoted. And when clarity is absent, confusion always fills the void. And what breeds confusion? Poor communication. Want to know what kills confusion? Open communication via 1-on-1 meetings.

That's what Matt felt like with Alex. Matt was a frequent flier on Sunday Scaries airlines. He had no idea where he stood with Alex. He was constantly fearful of losing his job. He wasn't sure if Alex liked him, supported him, or would ignore him on a street corner.

That was a problem. And as we've seen with the research, it's a problem your people (and likely even you yourself) are experiencing.

---

62 Joe Piskner, "Why People Get the 'Sunday Scaries'." The Atlantic, February 2020. https://www.theatlantic.com/family/archive/2020/02/sunday-scaries-anxiety-workweek/606289/

Additional Benefits

What we discussed above is important. But the benefits of 1-on-1 meetings don't end there. That's why we want to go through seven key, additional ways these meetings can impact your business.

Engagement

According to Gallup, just 36% of Americans are actively engaged in their jobs. However, the key to increasing that engagement is allowing employees to communicate weekly with their managers.[63] In other words, 1-on-1 meetings are directly linked to increased employee engagement, an important aspect we've talked about throughout this book.

Communication

Without effective communication, the rest of your leadership skills fall flat. While it seems simple, oral communication continues to appear on the top of the greatest skill shortage lists, especially in large cities such as Washington, D.C., San Francisco, and New York, making it an important skill to possess.[64] 1-on-1 meetings are a great time to work on your personal communication skills and develop them in your employees.

Body Language Matters

While the percentage and importance of non-verbal communication has come under scrutiny (it's not in the 90% range as many people like to say), the reality is that non-verbal cues are still wildly important.[65] The 1-on-1 meeting works well in this regard. In this setting, you and your employee can both read body language, reactions, and tone. That's why we suggest 1-on-1 meetings always

---

63 Jim Harter, "U.S. Employee Engagement Data Hold Steady in First Half of 2021" Gallup, July 2021. https://www.gallup.com/workplace/352949/employee-engagement-holds-steady-first-half-2021.aspx

64 Jacqui Barrett, "The U.S. is Facing a Critical Skills Shortage, Reskilling Can Be Part of the Solution." LinkedIn, April 2018. https://blog.linkedin.com/2018/april/19/the-u-s-is-facing-a-critical-skills-shortage-reskilling-can-be-part-of-the-solution

65 Jeff Thompson, "Is Nonverbal Communication a Numbers Game?". Psychology Today, September 2011. https://www.psychologytoday.com/us/blog/beyond-words/201109/is-nonverbal-communication-numbers-game

try to be done in person or include a video component.

Reinforce Culture & Vision (Alignment)

Most companies expect culture and vision to cascade down through large staff meetings or once-a-year offsites. Or worse yet, through osmosis. In reality, reinforcing culture and vision works best via regular 1-on-1 meetings that can consistently address misalignment. Your organization can become unstoppable when your company rallies around a single, unified mission and vision. And that's accomplished amidst a culture of feedback and effective 1-on-1 meetings.

Achieving Goals

Getting things done is the name of the game. It's a huge motivator for why we go to work every day. The best managers know the top priorities for each of their staff and take on a coaching role to effectively work with them to achieve their goals. The 1-on-1 meeting is the perfect format to tackle not only the "why" and the "what" but also the "how," acting as the consistent touchpoint to make sure employees hit outcomes.

Show you Care (Build Trust)

With constant changes at organizations and the busyness of our schedules, it's easy for team members to go unnoticed or feel left behind. 1-on-1s disrupt this tendency by keeping an authentic relationship in place. (Emphasis on the word "authentic.") The strongest teams have a leader that shows authentically who they are and that they care. Curt Cronin, former Navy SEAL and CEO of Ridgeline Partners, says, "People don't want work-fueled robots guiding their companies. They would much rather work for skilled, empathetic leaders who feel passionately about their missions, make honest mistakes and learn along the way."[66] That *must* be you.

---

66 Curt Cronin, "3 Ways Authentic Leaders Inspire and Retain Employees." Entrepreneur, February 2019. https://www.entrepreneur.com/leadership/3-ways-authentic-leaders-inspire-and-retain-employees/327220

Empowerment

One of the worst things in the workplace is a boss who refuses to give up control. And not many things can kill your company and drain it of skilled people like a boss who doesn't empower this around and under them.

Craig Groeschel puts it this way, and we think it's powerful: "When you delegate tasks, you create followers. When you delegate authority, you create leaders. The strength of your organization is not a reflection of WHAT you control but WHO you empower."[67]

Empowering your team will also provide great side effects, like creating a positive work environment, saving time, and raising the ceiling of your organization's potential.

A great time and place to begin that empowerment is actually in 1-on-1 meetings. It's where you can delegate, create, and dream. Think of it as the vehicle for delivering true empowerment.

HOW TO CONDUCT EFFECTIVE 1-ON-1 MEETINGS

So you've seen why 1-on-1 meetings are important. They create clarity and serve as the foundation of the alliance we've been talking about (among other things). But how do you actually conduct them? How do you implement them? Because there's a difference between simple 1-on-1 meetings and effective 1-on-1 meetings.

Remember our ROI statistic from earlier? Organizations realized a 529% ROI from regular 1-on-1 meetings, but only when those meetings were defined by consistent employee coaching.[68] This sacred time is not effective when both parties are simply

---

67 Craig Groeschel. "When you delegate tasks, you create followers." Facebook, January 23, 2021. https://www.facebook.com/craiggroeschel/photos/a.119436738114919/3776076965784193/?type=3

chit-chatting. Making 1-on-1 meetings effective really comes down to strategy.

Your strategy should consist of these four parts at a minimum:

- Format: specifically length and setting
- Frequency: consistency breeds trust because it shows you care
- Agenda: a tool to manage it, prepare for it, and ask the right questions
- Documentation: one place to look back on agenda items and notes and view progress

Below, we'll walk you through some working best practices, but be open to developing your own flow or style. Don't be afraid to make adjustments to your strategy as you go.

And if you're looking for clues on how to know if your 1-on-1 meetings are effective, look for these elements:

- Levels of engagement on your team are going up
- Problems are being solved faster
- Greater alignment both in culture and execution of work
- Increased open communication
- Measurable employee development

CHOOSING THE BEST FORMAT FOR YOUR 1-ON-1 MEETING

First things first: format. That's key. And that comes down to making a game plan. Here are some tips on the format.

68 Merrill Anderson, "Executive Briefing." (no. 2)

Length

1-on-1s should not be less than 20 minutes and rarely exceed 60 minutes. We've found that 45 minutes is actually the sweet spot. It's easy to keep track of three 15-minute increments, and it cuts down on wasted time and the pressure to fill an hour just because you feel like you have to.

For example:

- 15 minutes to catch up and ask a meaningful conversation question
- 15 minutes to cover day-to-day updates and priorities
- 15 minutes to go over action items and any coaching or feedback

Setting

This may seem like common sense, but many managers do not provide a safe and secure environment to have 1-on-1 meetings. Remember when Alex brought Matt to a Whole Foods? That wasn't a great setting. It showed that he was mailing it in right off the bat. Not compromising on setting shows your team you truly care. Spending an extra five minutes thinking about the setting can pay huge dividends. And a proper setting also breeds trust and candor in the conversation.

Some things to keep in mind:

- Typically, holding 1-on-1 meetings in a private office or conference room with the door closed makes the most sense. This limits interruptions and protects privacy.
- Other non-traditional options, like an off-site coffee shop or even a walk, also work. These types of meetings may be a better fit for your culture or current office space setup.
- What feels safe and secure to you may not feel safe or secure to your employee. Marcus Buckingham even goes so far as to suggest that, "To get the best coaching outcomes, always have your 1-on1s on your employee's

turf, not yours. In your office, the truth hides."[69]

The goal is to create a comfortable, safe, and secure environment conducive to honest and productive conversations.

Frequency

1-on-1 meetings will never be effective if they aren't conducted regularly. Regularity conveys importance; if you want your meetings to be effective, they must feel important.

The best industry leaders have 1-on-1 meetings with their subordinates once a week. Facebook's Mark Zuckerberg puts it this way: "[E]very week we start the week and end the week just meeting one-on-one together, and going over everything that's going on, and [reflecting], giving each other feedback."[70]

When Sharyl Sandberg joined Facebook, she explained how important those weekly check-ins are:

> "We always know that we're going to talk things through and we're going to get on the same page. And when we're not on the same page, we're going to keep talking it through. I do one-on-ones with the people working on my team, Mark does one-on-ones, and it reverses down. I think it's helped the company a lot."[71]

Not surprisingly, weekly 1-on-1 meetings help build a culture of trust, transparency, and consistency. And consistency ensures clarity among your team, as everyone knows what to expect. That contributes to the healthy culture that you want to create.

---

69 Rachel Thalmann, "The Truth Hides in Your Office: How to Get the Best Evaluation Outcomes." LinkedIn, March 2019. https://www.linkedin.com/pulse/truth-hides-your-office-rachel-thalmann/

70 Manuela Barcenas, "One-on-One Meeting Frequency: How Often Do Great Managers Meet With Their Direct Reports?" Fellow, March 2019. https://fellow.app/blog/meetings/one-on-one-meeting-frequency/

71 Manuela Barcenas, "One-on-One Meeting Frequency" (no. 13)

A caveat, though. Andy Grove, the former Intel CEO, believes each employee's level of experience and knowledge should dictate the frequency of 1-on-1 meetings. The more senior and directly involved in a project, the greater the frequency a manager should meet with this employee.[72]

Ultimately, the decision is yours and should reflect the stage of the company, your culture, and the pressing tasks at hand. We've even seen some companies ramp up the frequency to once a week to better handle a toxic culture or a complicated project, but then wind down to every other week. To start, we recommend implementing weekly meetings for at least a month before altering the cadence.

How to set the Agenda

With the number of competing priorities and the busyness of your schedule, it will be tempting to just "show up" to each 1-on-1 meeting. But preparation shows you take this concept seriously, and we can't stress the importance of that. "Winging it" by responding on the fly to comments, recalling projects off the top of your head, or expecting the employee to drive the bulk of the conversation and follow-up documentation afterward breeds resentment and disaster and leads to the opposite effect of what you're trying to achieve: trust and buy-in.

We can't stress this enough: You need to prepare!

Preparation doesn't have to eat up a huge amount of time; 15-30 minutes throughout the week should do it. At the very least, block out 10 minutes prior to each 1-on-1 meeting to review the agenda and prepare some questions. Ideally, both the manager and the employee will collaborate on the agenda ahead of the weekly meeting. In fact, that's one of the reasons we created Leadr – to give managers and employees a tool to plan meetings, take notes, and recap what was discussed.

---

72 Manuela Barcenas, "One-on-One Meeting Frequency" (no. 13)

When you're planning, remember our 15-minute format:

- Personal catch-up and meaningful conversation
- Review of top priorities and project updates
- Action items, next steps, and any coaching items

Additionally, work to incorporate the following types of content into your agendas:

- Past meeting discussions
- Feedback given or received
- Assessments
- Cultural or capability standards
- Content for learning
- Coaching or development plan progress
- Positive recognition and celebration

Initially, we recommend the manager to run the meetings and set the agendas. Eventually, help your employees mature by slowly giving them more and more of the meeting agenda. This can help them improve their confidence, preparation, and communication skills. Be sure to demonstrate the skills you want them to develop by doing it yourself early on.

Still, even though your employees may eventually drive these meetings, never ignore your role as coach. They still need to hear your feedback, encouragement, and direction. We suggest you, the manager, should always own the responsibility of creating a meaningful conversation each week. An easy way to do that is by using our list of predetermined 1-on-1 questions.[73]

Asking Great Questions

That leads us here. Just like good 1-on-1 meetings are foundational to people development, good questions are foundational to good 1-on-1 meetings. Good questions help you break down walls and dig beneath the surface of the canned answers employees are so used to giving. They create trust, they allow you to get to know the employee, and they ultimately create buy-in. The key is avoiding "yes or no" questions and asking open-ended ones.

We suggest preparing these open-ended questions ahead of time and sharing them with your direct reports before the meeting so there are no surprises. If they feel prepared, the conversation will be better. However, that shouldn't prevent you from asking follow-ups if you feel the answers are too canned. Demonstrate your genuine interest with the questions you ask.

Still, be sure to temper your reaction to their potentially negative or surprising answers. Non-verbal cues, as we've mentioned, speak volumes about whether you are a safe person. Are you actually committed to their development? Or is this just some new management ploy to weed out bad employees? You always want them to answer "yes" to the first question.

All of that assumes one important thing, though: You are going to listen. Don't formulate a response before you've heard them out. Don't think about the next question before you hear the answer to the previous one. Employees will pick up on this, making your 1-on-1 meetings less effective because it creates a lack of trust.

Here are a few additional suggestions to get you started.

Use ice-breaker questions to set the tone, such as:

1. What's been on your mind lately?
2. What motivates you to come to work each day?

---

73 You can find those here: http://leadr.com/one-on-one

3. If money were no object, what would you do every day?
4. What part of your job do you enjoy the most? And which part do you enjoy least?

Notice how those questions are open-ended. That's important. After that, move into day-to-day role questions (which can also be project-specific):

1. What roadblocks or frustrations do you have that I could help eliminate?
2. Is everyone pulling their weight on the team?
3. What could make your current project easier?

Lastly, show them that you "see" them with career-centered questions:

1. What are you doing really well that is helping you move toward your personal goals?
2. Are there any areas of your job in which you would like additional training?
3. Do you feel we're helping you advance your career at a pace you would like? Why or why not?

Finally, don't give up when it gets hard. We understand people management, and developing effective 1-on-1 meetings, requires a shift for a lot of people. Asking the right questions and demonstrating healthy responses takes practice. You will make mistakes and you may encounter situations beyond your leadership expertise. Be sure to find a mentor who can advise you as you simultaneously work on your growth.

But whatever you do, don't abandon the meetings. They are foundational to people management. Tweak? Yes. Abandon? Never.

MATT

THE RIGHT AMOUNT OF VULNERABILITY

We've alluded to vulnerability – and specifically the right amount of it – several times throughout this book, so I'm excited to finally break it down for you. We've made it clear that managers need to be vulnerable with their employees. It's an important part of building trust, which often happens during 1-on-1 meetings.

I'll repeat this: You need to be vulnerable with those who report to you. But how vulnerable? How much do you share? The answer can be tricky. The short answer is this: Be vulnerable enough to build trust, but guarded enough to protect you, the employee, and the business.

I've put my foot in my mouth a lot over the years when it comes to vulnerability. In general, I tend to be more of an open book than a closed one. In the interest of being "real," I've made flippant comments that come back to bite me. So here's what I've learned: The more senior your position, the more careful you have to be with how candid you are with your subordinates.

We've felt this tension a lot at Leadr. As a startup, things can go from good to bad very quickly. It's a constant roller coaster. For example, in the fall of 2022, the tech market (along with the market in general) took a nosedive. Everyone was talking about a recession, and we were trying to raise another round of funding right in the middle of it. Our numbers, not surprisingly, weren't where we wanted them.

So, in that season, if a young, concerned staff member walked into my office and asked me how the business was going, what would I have said? It probably would have sounded something like this:

"I completely understand your feelings. In fact, I think everyone should have some level of concern, considering what's going on worldwide. You wouldn't be human if you weren't concerned. As a company, we're definitely feeling some of the effects of the market. We're a tech company, after all. That's made fundraising a little harder. However, my commitment and the leadership team's commitment has never been stronger. We live for moments like this, which is why we got into the startup game. We see a path forward. But honestly, we really do need your help. We need everyone to give a little extra. If that happens, I have all the confidence in the world that we're on the cusp of something really special."

There are a few things I want to point out about that example.

First, it's good to start by validating someone's feelings. Whether you agree or not, the person coming to you with a concern still feels the way they're feeling. That doesn't mean you never offer new information that could change those feelings, but immediately dismissing them or launching into a lawyer-like argument about why they shouldn't feel that way rarely works. You can't verbally beat someone into feeling a different way, but you can gently educate them.[74]

Second, it's important to deal with reality. If I had said, "What are you talking about? Things are fine! There's absolutely nothing to worry about!" I would have immediately been discredited. After all, anyone can look at the stock market and see if the economy is in trouble. So it's important to find easy "honest wins," as I like to call them. These are easy ways to show honesty and vulnerability that don't go too far.

Third, it was important in this example to restate my resolve and the resolve of our leadership team. We're not looking for an easy exit. We're not looking to pack it in when it gets tough. We truly do live for these moments and stating

---

74 If you're married, you know this well. How many times have you been told, "I don't want you to fix it, I just want you to listen."

that is important. It gives confidence. "Yes, we know it's tough, but that will not ruin our resolve!"

Finally, the example concludes by calling the employee not just to recognize the problem but help solve it. This is a perfect way to encourage buy-in. It also solidifies so much of what we've talked about regarding inviting your people into the solution and empowering them to reach their full potential. In essence, it's the type of conversation I would have had with Amanda from the last chapter, when we were looking into a dark sales abyss and needed everyone to give a little more to ensure we didn't fall in.

So how might this conversation have been different with someone more senior? I'm glad you asked. If my director of marketing had come in and asked me the same question, someone who is my direct report, here's how I would have responded:

"You're right to be concerned. We all need to be. We're a tech startup, and the market is not good right now. Investors and potential investors are skittish. But every moment of worry I've had has been with an equal amount of confidence. And part of that has to do with you and your team. I truly believe that our future will come down, in big part, to how you and the team step up. And I know you can. I've seen you do it before. So I would love to see a plan that really shores up our budget while also coming up with inventive ways to spread our message. And know that I'm in this with you. We all need to go above and beyond right now, including me. If we do, I believe we'll be around for a long time. But also, if something bad does happen, know that you are a valuable member of this organization and we're going to take care of you."

Notice the uptick in vulnerability in the second example. With the newer staff member, I was vulnerable but guarded. With my director of marketing, I was still guarded – I didn't share the animated conversations I had with the board, for example – but gave her even more information and candor. That's important. In the end, vulnerability builds trust. But 100% vulnerability with no filter can destroy your morale, your reputation, and your organization. Employees want their leaders to be vulnerable, for sure, but they also have to be motivated to follow them into battle.

One of the best examples I've seen of this is in the classic tale, *The Lord of the Rings*. In the final installment, *The Return of the King*, the armies of Rohan face the impossible task of taking on the seemingly insurmountable army of Sauron. As the Rohirrim prepare for what seems like their inevitable death, the men express doubt about the task. They've lost hope. That's when Theoden, King of Rohan and their leader in battle, speaks up.

"We cannot defeat the armies of Mordor," Gamling, one of his lieutenants, says.

"No, we cannot," Theoden replies. "But we will meet them in battle nonetheless." When he delivers that line, in the movie, you see a cadre of soldiers in the background nod their heads in support. [75]

That confidence eventually helped inspire the defeat of Sauron in the ultimate battle of good vs. evil. Why? I think partly because Theoden simultaneously recognized the reality of the situation while calling his men to something greater. And it paid off.

You need to be Theoden.

The following example will help you figure out exactly what to share and what not to share in your quest to be both guarded and vulnerable. When it comes to this interplay, Chris and I take a cascading approach to vulnerability. What

---

75 The Lord of the Rings: The Return of the King. DVD. New Line Cinema, 2003.

does that look like?

I'm 100% vulnerable with my wife.

I'm 95% vulnerable with Chris.

I'm 80% vulnerable with my leadership team.

And I'm about 60% vulnerable with the wider company.

Those are good numbers to start with for yourself. They help protect you, your employees, and your company. At the end of the day, it's impossible to give all of yourself to all people at all times. As you interact with employees (and even friends) with whom you don't have as deep of a relationship, you have to hold a certain part of yourself back. If you vomit on everyone, it's not long before you get dehydrated.

But the other reason you should wisely hold back is not for you but for those around you. If you were, for example, to bare your soul to a sales director, while that may be cathartic, it could be dangerous because they don't have the knowledge and context you have. If I bare my soul to Chris, he has the context to digest that information, not just professionally but personally. He can "chew the meat and spit out the bones," as the saying goes.

But if I pour out my soul and all the problems the company is facing to someone I may only interact with once a month or even once a week, they don't have that context. They don't have vital information to "take it with a grain of salt."

For example, while writing this book, my grandfather died. That was tough for me. We were in the middle of some stressful times at work, yet I had to fly back to New Zealand to attend the funeral, be with my family, and grieve. If a younger staff member had asked me how I was doing and I told them, "Well, my grandpa just died, the market is crashing, and I'm honestly feeling a little burned out at the moment trying to juggle it all," that would have been detrimental to morale. It would have raised a lot of questions. They would have gone home and told their spouse, "I just talked to Matt and he's not doing well. I think the company is in trouble. He used the phrase 'burnt out.' I think I should start looking for another job." And you can bet that sentiment would have spread throughout the company.

However, if I shared that same sentiment with Chris, he would have comforted me, encouraged me, and wouldn't have, for a second, lost faith in my ability to lead. He knows that in times of stress, I tend to make more sweeping statements that may feel real at the moment but, with time, actually diminish. Because he has the luxury of relationship and context.

In the end, there are times when I tell certain people what's really happening with the company and with me, and there are times when I mince my words.

Because the difference between good transparency and bad transparency is finding who to be appropriately transparent with and then determining the right amount.

CHAPTER 7

GIVING EFFECTIVE FEEDBACK

MATT

I'm not going to lie. I was frustrated. Upset may even be the better term.

We were at a day-long, off-site meeting. I had started suspecting things weren't as rosy as the managers reporting to me had been saying.[76] So I did something a little different. Throughout the day, I began grabbing people out of the room for 15-20 minutes at a time. I would ask them some simple questions.

"How's it going, really?"

"How's your relationship with your manager?"

"Are you getting consistent feedback?"

I knew full well what the honest answers should be. I had begun getting little nuggets here or there suggesting that, even though we were a people

---

76 By the way, this is a good lesson for leaders: The higher up the ladder you climb, the more naturally disconnected you will get from what's happening on the front lines. And the more mid-level managers you'll encounter who like to hide or twist the truth to cover up mistakes.

development company, some in our ranks weren't exactly practicing what we were preaching.

But I didn't fully expect Sheila to tell me what she did.

"Matt, this is a little hard for me to say because I'm not looking to get anyone in trouble. But you asked, so I'm just going to be honest," she said. "Matt, I haven't gotten any actual feedback from my boss in the last 18 months."

My jaw hit the floor. I kept my cool, but inside, my frustration skyrocketed.

"Really? I'm so sorry to hear that. Can you explain a little more?" I asked.

"All I've been told is that I'm doing an amazing job," she continued, "and that I just need to keep it up. But I haven't heard anything constructive. I haven't heard anything that can make me better. And because of that, I feel like I'm stagnant."

I thanked Sheila for her candor and courage. And it wasn't long before I confronted her boss. In that conversation, I made something very clear: It's not enough to have consistent meetings. You have to be giving effective feedback in those meetings. And effective feedback is constructive in nature.

We've said that today's workforce wants to be invested in. Do you know one of the most effective ways to invest in someone? Giving them constructive feedback.

I know it may sound counterintuitive, but your high performers (which Sheila was) aren't sitting around thinking, "I just wanna be told how amazing I am." By definition, high performers are constantly looking to improve. To grow. And if you deprive them of that, you'll lose them.

That had happened earlier in the year. We lost a high performer – one of Sheila's colleagues – who was working under the same manager. And when I talked to the manager about why, I got a lot of excuses, but nothing that felt like it was based in reality. That's why I went directly to Sheila. And what I found out shocked me.

We talked in the last chapter about how 1-on-1 meetings create clarity. And that's true. But they only create clarity when real, honest feedback is present. In this example, Sheila wasn't looking to be told how awesome she was at every turn. She's smart, so she knew there were things she could improve on. But her manager was cheating her out of that growth, stifling her and eroding her buy-in.

Sheila's manager was conducting regular 1-on-1 meetings. That wasn't the problem. But just like Alex in the last chapter, her manager was simply checking the box. He was completing the task but missing the point: giving effective feedback.

Defining Effective Feedback

We said in Chapter 6 that where clarity is absent, confusion fills the void. That's an important reminder here. If an employee doesn't know where they stand with a manager, their imagination usually fills the void with something far worse than reality.

"They gave me a weird look the other day. I'm probably getting fired," they'll say. That's what happened to Alex and me. His absence left me filling the void with those types of thoughts the day he invited me to lunch for the first time.

As a manager, then, it's imperative that you fill the void with reality by giving consistent feedback that produces clarity via 1-on-1 meetings.

I don't pretend this is always easy.

You might think, "Matt, you've been telling me this new workforce wants to feel included. If I give constructive feedback and tell an employee, for example, that they need to work on something, won't I alienate them?"

Sharing constructive feedback can feel awkward, for sure. You may feel like sharing with someone about how they can improve will create relational withdrawal or break trust. And in fact, you may even think that outright withholding hard feedback is protecting the employee, who may be going through a hard time personally. I get those feelings; I really do.

But I'm here to tell you that the employees you want to keep around at your company – the ones who are going to turbo your business – are the ones that, despite the surrounding noise and circumstances, want hard feedback. They want to learn and to grow. Like Sheila, they don't want to be constantly told how awesome they are. That's the misconception.

Here's the beauty of hard feedback: While it may not be easy in the moment, it's best in the long run. Best for the employee, best for you, and best for the business. If done correctly, it always creates better employees, better managers, and better companies. And by giving hard feedback, you're telling your employee, "I believe in you enough to have hard conversations." Because, in the end, you don't give hard feedback to people you don't care about. That's true in life, and it's true in business. You value those you have hard conversations with.

That means the best employees are the ones that live for those types of conversations. Because they understand tough conversations create trust and growth.

I'll say it clearly and plainly: If you want to be an effective leader, you have to give constructive, and at times hard, feedback. And if you want to be an effective employee that's constantly developing, you have to welcome that feedback as well.

CHRIS AND MATT

THE SEVEN RULES OF EFFECTIVE FEEDBACK

So you understand that feedback is important. But how do you actually do it? What does it look like to put it into practice? Where do you start? Well, we've developed seven rules for understanding and implementing effective feedback. These rules are based on our experience at Pushpay and the culture we've created at Leadr, and we think they will help you take a big step toward creating a vibrant feedback culture.

Number 1: Effective Feedback is Constructive Feedback

This one is important, which is why we gave it its own section above. That's because you have to first understand what something is before you can implement it. And if effective feedback is constructive feedback, that means withholding hard feedback is more detrimental to someone's growth than actually telling them the truth. That doesn't mean you need to set out to verbally destroy an employee with hard truth (which we'll cover in a bit), but you can't shy away from it.

(And if you're struggling to envision what hard feedback looks like or how to go about it, we'll show you in just a bit.)

Number 2: Intent Matters

"Feedback is not about sizing people up," author and leadership expert Adam Grant explains. "It's about helping them grow."[77]

---

77 Adam Grant, "Feedback is not about sizing people up." Facebook, October 19, 2022. https://www.facebook.com/photo.php?fbid=673719914115869&set=pb.100044335993931.-2207520000.&type=3

When people ask us how to give effective feedback, we first tell them that you have to go into it with the right intent. That's why we love the above quote from Adam Grant. If the intent of your feedback is to berate, belittle, or bemoan, it will never be effective. But if the goal is to help the person grow, to develop them along the lines that they have laid out via their personal development plan, to forge and grow the alliance, that's when it becomes effective. Never go into a 1-on-1 looking to punish someone. Always approach it with the understanding that you're both there to learn.

Number 3: It has to be Consistent

Recently, Matt's friend Carrie got a call from a colleague who was in tears. That colleague had just gotten some tough feedback. But that's not exactly why she was crying.

"Annie just had a terrible performance review," Carrie said in a text. "She scored below average on one of the categories because of customer feedback that came in six months ago, which hadn't been shared with her. She also got feedback about three other things that were a complete surprise. I'm helping her clean up her resume because she's looking for a different job ASAP. I might do the same."

Carrie's colleague wasn't upset at the feedback, per se. She was upset that her manager had never brought it up in a previous meeting. Managers, the feedback you give during an annual performance review should never surprise your employee. Never. If you are following the foundations of people development and truly care about your employees, you should be giving them consistent feedback, both good and bad. It also helps you as a leader and as a business. When you withhold feedback, you're robbing the employee and the company of growth. When you give it, you're helping both get better.

It shouldn't shock you that the best way to be consistent with feedback is via

1-on-1 meetings. That's why we covered that concept in the previous chapter. If you're regularly having 1-on-1 meetings, you will naturally be consistent with your feedback.

Number 4: It has to be Timely

You cannot withhold feedback. Said another way, your feedback has to be timely. Especially as it relates to hard feedback, it has to be given as close to the incident or decision as possible. Once again, regular 1-on-1 meetings create those opportunities.

Just look at the above text from Carrie again. It wasn't that her colleague got hard feedback. It was that her manager – absent any 1-on-1 meetings – withheld it from her for so long and then surprised her with it. The apparent incident was now six months away, meaning there couldn't be a productive conversation about it. And that eroded trust. So much so that not only was she starting to look for another job, but it was so frustrating that Carrie began wondering if she should start polishing her resume, too.

It's a perfect example of how withholding feedback can ruin morale and culture and push your high performers away.

So when is the best time to give feedback? Researcher Todd A. Thornock studied just that. When comparing the amount of time that passes without receiving feedback to future performance, he found the most beneficial time to give feedback is shortly after a decision (or action) is made. In other words, the more timely an employee receives feedback, the more quickly their performance will improve. Here's how Thornock says it:

> When feedback is provided before implementation of an initial decision, high learning costs discourage individuals from learning in the initial period to the detriment of future performance. Further, when feedback

is provided after extended delays beyond implementation of a decision, learning costs increase relative to those present when feedback is provided after a short delay, resulting in lower learning and future performance. As such, I find that providing feedback immediately following implementation of a decision most effectively promotes learning and future performance as this is the point at which learning costs are lowest.[78]

The caveat in that first sentence is key, too. You can give feedback too quickly. You can stifle innovation by shooting something down before an employee can try it. That's a form of micromanagement, and it's a culture killer.

In the end, don't give feedback too soon or give it too late. Be timely about it.

Number 5: It Should be Specific

One surefire way to kill a good feedback session is to make it general. Phrases like, "You're just not cutting it," or, "You need to do better," aren't really helpful. They're too broad and don't give an employee anything actionable. That's why feedback has to be specific.

Here are two better examples:

- "I'm noticing you've been late to work five out of the last seven days. Can you help me understand what's going on?"
- "Your sales numbers are down 20% month over month. What do you attribute that to?"

In the same way, you, as a manager, need to ask for specific feedback wherever possible. Leadership guru Craig Groeschel says it perfectly:

---

78 Todd Thornock, "How the Timing of Performance Feedback Impacts Individual Performance." *Accounting, Organizations and Society* 55. (May 2016): 1-11. https://www.sciencedirect.com/science/article/abs/pii/S0361368216300770#!

"Have any feedback for me?" is a terrible question to start with. General questions rarely lead to specific answers. General questions rarely lead to specific feedback. You're going to hear some things you don't like. When that happens, don't get defensive. Instead, train yourself to say things like "Tell me more" or "Help me understand."[79]

For example, instead of asking someone, "How was my talk?" Ask them, "How did I do with my hands during that speech?" That goes a long way to improving your public speaking because it's actionable.[80]

Number 6: It Should be Tailored

As a leader, you are responsible for tailoring your feedback to the person you're giving it to. Feedback preference is going to differ from employee to employee. That doesn't mean you have to be walking on eggshells all the time, but you owe it to your people to understand their communication style. That's why we stressed getting to know your employees so much in the earlier chapters.

Remember the section on personal development plans? There was a reason it involved a survey question about how the employee likes to receive feedback. Some people like you to get straight to the point. Others will prefer a "feedback sandwich," where you start with praise, give constructive criticism, and then end with another thing they've been doing well. That's not wrong; that's just them.

CHRIS

You also have to ensure you're offering feedback at the right time. We've talked about the importance of giving it sooner rather than later, but you also have to exercise wisdom. If you know someone who just got some tough news at home,

---

79 Craig Groeschel, "Giving and Receiving Feedback, Part 1." Leadership Podcast. December 2017. https://open.life. church/training/332-craig-groeschel-leadership-podcast-giving-and-receiving-feedback-part-1

80 This same concept of pursuing specificity is also good to keep in mind when setting or discussing goals.

that might not be the right day to give them feedback on their most recent presentation. That doesn't mean you withhold it completely. It just means you give it when they can actually receive it in the best way possible.

My wife and I have learned the value of getting feedback at the right time and place. Because of that, we started a tradition called "Serious Sundays." The idea is that we reserve really hard conversations and topics for a specific time on Sundays. We can each prepare and give each other more attention and grace during those times. You know what "Serious Sundays" are called in the business world? 1-on-1 meetings.

If you've done the pre-work of getting to know your people well, it makes this rule – and threading the needle – that much easier.

MATT

Number 7: Don't be a Jerk

While we are huge advocates for not shying away from tough conversations, that doesn't mean you have a license to be mean, rude, or belittling.

Consider this: A friend of mine once told me about some awful feedback she got from her manager. She went into an important meeting with the leadership team and, as it went on, she began to passionately defend her perspective. At one point, her manager interrupted her with a statement.

"You're too animated," her manager said.

"Excuse me?" my friend replied.

"You're too animated," the manager repeated.

Needless to say, my friend was devastated. Why? Not because she didn't want to know how she was coming across, but because of how that feedback was delivered. My friend immediately felt attacked, belittled, and personally dismissed or flawed.

She told me later: "I thought, 'I'm too animated? I've brought in millions of dollars for your company by being who I am and you're telling me that I'm too animated?'"

We're not saying that feedback didn't need to be shared. It just didn't need to be shared like that. A better way would have been to say something like, "Hey, I can tell you're really passionate about this topic and I'm really grateful that you are because I know you care about our company. But the way you're communicating right now, I'm unable to truly hear you. What about trying a different way or coming back to the conversation a little later?"

See the difference?

As I unpacked the conversation with my friend, she clarified that she appreciated the sentiment behind her boss's feedback. Still, she wasn't able to get there until days later, when she had waded through the slog of how it was delivered. That's an important lesson. If you're delivering your feedback poorly, your employees are much less likely to take it and use it. And that defeats the purpose.

That's why all of these rules are important. They set you up for success and ensure the time you're spending is paying off. Follow them, and we guarantee that delivering feedback will not only become easier but also begin paying dividends.

CHRIS AND MATT

NAVIGATING DIFFICULT CONVERSATIONS

There is one key aspect we've talked about so far that requires further explanation. It's the reality that if effective feedback is constructive, you'll inevitably encounter difficult conversations requiring more care.

In fact, research has found that no matter where someone falls in a generational data group, everyone wants feedback – even if it's hard to hear sometimes: 90% of millennials want candid, frequent feedback, along with 85% of GenY and 71% of GenX.[81]

That means you're naturally going to have more difficult conversations with employees. And while the seven rules mentioned above form the basis of delivering effective feedback in general, we want to equip you to specifically navigate the conversations on the tougher end of the spectrum.

Start with this: Challenging conversations don't have to burn bridges. In fact, when done well, these conversations can actually become learning opportunities that build more trust instead of eroding it.

With that in mind, here are some specific tips for navigating difficult conversations, no matter who they're between or what the issue is. You'll notice that many of them build on the foundational principles we just covered:

Improvement, Not Punishment
When you sit down to deliver difficult feedback to someone, keep the proper end goal in mind: improvement. The person you're talking to needs to feel that

---

81 Carolyn Edgecomb, "The Power and Importance of Negative Feedback for Employees." Impact Plus, 2016. https://www.impactplus.com/blog/importance-of-negative-feedback-for-employees

the desired outcome is not just to repair or criticize whatever went wrong, but to help build healthier patterns that move their development forward. Treat it like a partnership where the goal is to grow. Questions like, "What can we do differently next time?" will make it feel like this is for their ultimate good, not a punishment for messing up.

Keep it Timely and Relevant

While it can be tempting (especially in the heat of the moment) to reference numerous examples of previous mistakes or habitual bad practices, it's generally best to address the situation at hand. This breaks down defensiveness, helps the person hear what isn't working, and identifies a clear path toward improvement and growth.

With that said, if you've noticed a pattern emerging, it can be both beneficial and necessary to point that out. If this happens, it's still important to be as targeted as possible and not act like an attack dog or prosecutor. The ultimate focus should be on giving the employee timely, specific feedback, and then identifying a manageable action item they can start working on to improve right away.

Also, you may have noticed the word "timely" again. If your employee has made a mistake, waiting months or even weeks to bring it up will create hostility, erode trust, and make the conversation even more difficult. It's poor leadership and bad business.

Have a Conversation

We used an important word in the second point above: partnership. Be clear that you're working together to improve what's happened or what's happening. Have a conversation about what's going on. Even though the issue may indeed be the employee's fault, heaping unnecessary blame or guilt on them isn't helpful. In fact, they may not even recognize the problem to begin with. That's why asking how the person felt they performed in the situation is important.

There are some conversation starters we regularly use to help with this aspect. They are ways to ease into hard feedback conversations that work toward change:

- "Do you mind if I challenge you a little on something?"
- "How might that not have been ideal in this situation?"
- "Is there anything you think you could have done better?"
- "I have some feedback I'd like to share that I think will really help you."
- "In light of helping you towards your goal of X, I've been thinking about a specific area of growth that I feel is worth talking about."
- "Thanks for sharing that. I have some thoughts, but I'm curious what you think is a healthy resolution first."

Taking the time to ask for your employee's perspective allows them to get ahead of the issue when possible, solidifies the idea of a partnership, and leads to greater buy-in.

In the end, your job is walking alongside your employees and developing them. And the only way you'll ever get there is by having a conversation. By talking with them, not at them.

Document it

Although it can feel scary to document difficult conversations, doing so is critical to track growth and development. Offering a written history acts as a game plan for growth, creates alignment and clarity, and allows your team members something to reference.

Additionally, when the person does improve based on your feedback, having a written record allows you to look back and celebrate growth. Conversely, if changes don't happen, you need a reference point to remind them of the times you've worked to address it. (We'll also state the obvious here: Documenting tough conversations also gives you a reference for any future HR needs should you have to part ways with the employee.)

Remember, you never want feedback to feel like a surprise, so keeping track of it is a great way to create clarity and mitigate shock. This point is why, when we built the Leadr platform, we created an area to document and reference feedback. However, you can also document your conversations by sending a recap email to the employee and asking them to confirm what you discussed.

Avoid Absolutes

What's true in relationships is often true in work culture. You've probably heard the phrase, "Don't use absolutes," when discussing hard conversations in your personal life. The same rings true here. There's nothing that shuts down a conversation or puts people on the defensive quicker than telling them they "always" do something. Why? Because it's rarely true 100% of the time. Using an absolute, then, erodes trust.

Think about it. Is it really true that your employee is "always" late? Is it really true that they "never" follow through? Is it really true that they don't care "at all?" Probably not. And if you devolve into absolutes, you'll rarely find yourself having a productive conversation.

Create a Plan of Action

Feedback should always involve providing a solution to the problem. Most people don't display negative behaviors or results intentionally; they simply don't have the tools to help them develop in the areas where they may not be naturally skilled. Developing someone means offering tools and practical solutions for improvement.

At Leadr, we do this in our platform by setting goals for ourselves and team members. Goals, as we've discussed, can have more granular tasks associated with them to offer a consistent visual of the exact steps for improvement. Remember, clarity and alignment is critical for growth.

Follow up

Ensure you follow up after difficult feedback conversations. Follow-up can be the difference in increasing or decreasing buy-in. If you don't spend the time afterward, your employees will think you either don't truly care or don't take it seriously. Both are detrimental.

Following up also helps you celebrate successes and identify recurring weaknesses. If an employee continues to fall short, once again, make sure to document it while continuing to offer solution-based coaching.

Ask for Feedback Yourself

Leading by example is a powerful tool. Showing your own dedication to receiving feedback as a leader – and making clear it's a two-way conversation – builds trust. And when trust is earned, you'll create an environment where employees will eventually seek hard feedback from you proactively, knowing you have the tools to help them improve and grow. Once again, though, ask for specifics to make the conversation productive. Things like, "How am I doing at equipping you to do your job?" Or, "In what ways can I improve my communication?"

You'll get better answers if you ask better questions.

***

Remember, negative feedback isn't necessarily a bad thing. Caring for and developing your staff means having difficult conversations that help your team members identify areas of growth. While this isn't easy, it's necessary for long-term success. And it's worth the challenge.

CHRIS

CREATING A CULTURE OF FEEDBACK

Do you want to know the worst time to get feedback as a manager? It's after an employee has left. There have been times in my life when I've read a review on the anonymous company review site Glassdoor, for example, and been absolutely crushed.

Not only did the specific feedback throw me for a loop, but every time I'm left thinking, "How much did we fail this person, where they felt the only time and forum that they could give us feedback was anonymously after they left?" When you're getting the most critical feedback about your company on Glassdoor, there's a larger problem. It shows you that you don't have a culture of feedback, which ultimately points to a trust problem.

The goal, then, is to create a natural environment for people to feel like they can share where they're really at. The word "create" assumes it will take some work. That's because it will. We didn't always do this well in the early years of Pushpay, and we have to work at it every day at Leadr.

So how do you do that?

Whether you're giving or receiving it, feedback can be challenging to navigate – but it can also be transformative. Effective results start with asking the right questions. What did we do well? What can we work on? What can you learn from this? What will you do differently next time?

That last question might be the most important because it goes straight to the heart of why feedback is important. It's an open doorway to growth. If you are giving or receiving feedback without growth on either end, it's time for a reset.

So here are five ways to cultivate a feedback culture that focuses on growth:

Talk About it... a lot

If feedback is one of the most critical catalysts to growth and change, then you have to prop it up every chance you get.[82] Bring it up in meetings, work it into onboarding, discuss it at company events. Repeat the importance and value of feedback as often as possible so your people can see how much you value it. If you do that, they'll take it with them as a core part of your company's values.

Practice it

This tip may seem self-explanatory, and yet too many people talk about important things but fail to act on them. Learning to give and get good feedback is a habit. You might have to work at it until it becomes natural. One practical way we practice feedback at Leadr is to ask for it from team members after every meeting and presentation. This provides a safe space for people to share insights they might have glossed over previously. Thoughtfully sharing what you learned or what questions you have will lead to better discussions and deeper reflections, which are key parts of good feedback. It could also look like immediately pointing out a highlight of something someone did well or ensuring it's an agenda item in every 1-on-1 meeting.

Define it

You have to define your terms. What do you mean by feedback? Some people will provide a word and some will provide a novel. Explicitly spelling out what feedback should look like in your organization sets you and your team up for success. As you work to define feedback for your team, communicate it clearly. Also, remember that it might take some time to land on a definition and process that works for your company. But growth, not perfection, is the goal.

---

82 Leadr has a free workbook that you can use to level-up your feedback. It can be found here: https://www.leadr.com/small-progress-continuous-growth

Keep it Simple

This is important because good feedback should be clear, easy to understand, and to the point. Avoid feedback that's too long or belabored. You'll lose people's attention otherwise. At Leadr, here's what we keep in mind in order to keep feedback concise:

- Write bullet points, not novels.
- Spend thoughtful time but don't spend hours.
- Give feedback as you see it. As we've mentioned, for feedback to be effective, it must be timely. Discussing goals or performance a few times a year isn't enough. It should be an ongoing conversation.
- When providing feedback on a presentation or meeting, focus on the big ideas: what stood out, what you learned, what you disagreed with, what confused you, and what you would change.

Have a Good Attitude

Giving feedback can be hard, and getting it can be even harder. Keep in mind that feedback should always point back to growth. So while it might be hard to hear in the moment, the intention you need to communicate is that it's crucial for growth, leadership, development, job satisfaction, quality, and results. Those are good things! And yet, if we begrudgingly tackle giving and accepting feedback, you'll communicate the opposite. So be sure that the way you communicate – both verbally and nonverbally – conveys that you truly see the benefits. Your people will follow your lead.

MATT

MINING FOR CONFLICT

Chris's tips for creating a culture of feedback are good. And they remind me of another important point: Leaders have to mine for conflict. It's a staple of a healthy feedback culture.

We've already talked about how important it is for leaders to model the idea of giving and receiving feedback, but I want to take it a step further. One of the goals of giving and requesting feedback is to mine for conflict. That doesn't mean you're trying to stir up controversy or drama. But the reality in every organization is that there is more conflict than you can see. There's always more going on below the surface. And the healthiest organizations are constantly trying to bring that to light.

For example, I recently spoke with one of our sales leads who said we were suffering from "mission drift."

"When I joined a year ago, I knew what the mission was," he told me. "I could see it being lived out on a daily basis. But today, as things stand, I'm not sure I can see the mission being lived out as much as it was a year ago. We've had good people leave or get fired. I've missed out on several promotions. And because of that, I'm not sure we're really a people development company."

That was a lot to hear. But instead of getting defensive, I pressed into the conflict. I mined for it. Why? Because several assumptions were being made in this employee's statement that needed to be fleshed out. I realized that he would quit if I didn't press into this conversation. And he told me as much.

So I asked him about expectations. I asked him how he thought his performance was contributing to the mission. And then I continued to dig in, not in an argumentative way, but in an attempt to truly understand him and his experience before I even tried to "fix" what was going on.

At the end of the conversation, we reached an understanding. This employee got more context for some of the decisions that were made, I was able to offer him real feedback on his performance (which wasn't as stellar as he thought it was), and we got rid of several elephants in the room. He didn't end up leaving and actually leveled up personally. All because I didn't shy away from a tough conversation and mined for conflict.

So, here are some questions I use to mine for conflict that you can incorporate into your organization as well:

- "How are you treated on a regular basis?"
- "If your boss were to give me feedback about you, what do you think they would say?"
- "When was the last time you received feedback?"
- "What are you expecting to hear in your next performance review?"
- "What do you think you could be doing better?"

Those open-ended questions are powerful at bringing discontentment and unmet expectations to light. And just like in a relationship, unmet expectations are one of the most detrimental things in any organization. You need to root it out.

One final point. In creating a culture of feedback, you have to empower others in your organization to mine for conflict as well. Your HR team should regularly meet with individuals and ask them important questions like the ones above. In fact, a healthy HR team shouldn't constantly be putting out house fires, but should be proactively looking for matches to snuff out before they set the block ablaze.

CHRIS

THE ULTIMATE GOAL

So how do you know when you're getting it right? How do you know that you've created a culture of feedback and that your people have bought in? In my experience, the organizations that embody this the best have one thing in common: Employees and managers alike don't wait for feedback to come to them. They seek it out.

That's because the ultimate goal is to get your company to the point where everyone craves feedback. They're active when it comes to feedback, not passive.

While 1-on-1 meetings create a natural environment for feedback to occur, in a truly healthy, feedback-rich organization, people are constantly seeking it out. In those environments, people can't wait for their next 1-on-1 to know where they stand.

Now, that doesn't mean that if everyone in your organization isn't stopping each other in the halls and asking for feedback on their latest presentation, you have a bad feedback culture. But I will say, when it's so baked into your organization's DNA, the 1-on-1 meeting becomes the bare minimum cadence for getting feedback. It happens naturally in so many ways in between those meetings.

That's what we hope for you. We hope that you have so modeled and cultivated this concept that people can't wait to hear how they're doing and where they stand. And when that happens, we guarantee the results – the increased sales, the growth, and the winning – will follow.

MATT

WHEN YOU GET IT WRONG

I don't pretend that I've always nailed the feedback game. As Chris said above, it takes practice. And I've had a lot of practice.

But when (not if) you get it wrong, you have to own that. I've learned that the hard way.

During my two-and-a-half-year period as a VP of sales at Pushpay, I had 208 people either get fired or quit under my leadership. 208. That's a lot of people. In fact, if you do the math, that meant, on average, I was losing nearly two people a week. And while there are plenty of factors that contributed to that, when I stepped back and evaluated what went on, I realized that I was not effectively communicating with my people.

When I was preparing to leave Pushpay, I did something a little unconventional. I asked HR to print out a list of every single one of those 208 people. I then went through and circled all the names that left on bad terms.

You know what I did? I reached out and apologized. I reached out and owned what I could. Sure, maybe I wasn't at fault for everything. But in being honest with myself, I realized there was a lot I could own.

Why? Because my personal mission statement comes down to one word: reconcile. That means repairing what is broken. And I left too many broken people in my wake while I learned the lessons in this chapter and this book.

I wish I could say that everyone responded with excitement. They didn't. But they did all accept my apology.

You're going to mess up. You're not going to get feedback right. You're not going to get a lot of other things right. But the measure of a good leader is how well you accept responsibility when you get it wrong. That's also the measure of a mature person.

If you do that, you'll actually build trust in the wake of mistakes. You'll actually build morale. You'll actually build relationships. I need you to hear that. And then I need you to act on it.

EPILOGUE

GOING FORWARD

CHRIS

There's something that, when I first explain it to people, creates puzzled looks. It's this: A-grade employees will actually take up more of your time than B-grade employees.

Did you crinkle your nose a little? I thought you might. It's true though. Most people think it's the opposite, but it's not. Let me give you an example.

Let's say I come to a B-grade employee and ask them to build me a house. The employee agrees and gets to work quickly. Nine months later, they show up to my office and say, "Your house is done! Let's take a look."

So we go to the new house and, as I begin to survey it, I realize some problems.

"You used wood siding for the outside, but I really wanted brick," I say.

As we walk in, I notice something else. "How many bedrooms does it have?" I ask.

"Three," the B-grade employee responds.

"I wanted five."

"But did you see the countertops?"

"I did," I add. "But they're granite. I wanted quartz."

On and on it goes. So what was the problem? Technically, the B-grade employee completed the task and gave me a house. But the employee didn't give me what I wanted. Why?

Before I answer, consider how an A-grade employee would have handled that assignment. After I asked them to build me a house, the first thing that employee would have done was ask me some important questions.

- What kind of house?
- What do you want it to be built out of?
- How many bedrooms?
- What kind of countertops?

See the difference? A-grade employees take the time to seek clarity and get alignment. They pick your brain. They want your feedback. They set up a plan. They check in frequently. They crave more information.

And do you know what all of that takes? More time. More of their time, but also more of your time.

That's what I mean by A-grade employees taking more of your time than B-grade ones. However, it's a good tradeoff. Even though you're giving more of your time, the results are much better because they're what you want. Any builder can construct a house. They can throw something together and get it done. But the best builders – the best employees – take more of your time because they want to – they need to – get it right.

However, I don't like to think of it as them taking my time. I like to think of it as me investing in them. We made an alliance, and an alliance requires more from both parties. That, folks, is people development.

That little anecdote perfectly sums up what's going to be expected of you as you pivot towards people development and away from people management. It's going to require more upfront work. But it's work that pays dividends by forging the alliance we've talked about and ensuring you and your company get exactly what you need.

It's also a perfect example of the way you want your employees to act as they grow along with you. You want them to ask questions. You want them to crave feedback. You want them to prioritize alignment over their to-do list.

Next Steps

In the end, people management is a process. While you should take immediate steps to implement it, understand it will take time to turn the ship. Your goal as a new people developer needs to be to stay the course, no matter the waves, reefs, or winds that try to dissuade you.

So what are those small steps you can take immediately? Here are four:

- Inform and seek buy-in from your superiors. That may look like sending them this book to help them see the benefits, for example. But let them know you're trying something different and that they can and should ask you about the results.
- Start holding 1-on-1 meetings asap. While buy-in from the top is important, you don't need a board meeting to start implementing your own 1-on-1s. However, be sure to explain to your employees what you're

doing so you can get their buy-in as well.

- Ask your direct reports (via your 1-on-1 meetings) what they want to get from their time at your company. Have the conversation that starts forging the alliance.

- Ask for feedback. Even before you begin handing out feedback like candy, ask for it first. That sets the tone, creates the necessary culture, and creates curiosity as you model what you want others to do.

These four small things are a great gateway for pivoting towards a people development model. And the best thing is, they are completely up to you. Even though we want you to get buy-in, these steps don't require buy-in from the top to get going.[83]

As you implement them, keep track of metrics. Maybe that's sales numbers, maybe that's productivity goals, or maybe it's a unique performance metric your business uses. Whatever it is, track the before and after. And then, be prepared to discuss the results with your employees and bosses.

CHRIS AND MATT

DON'T FALL INTO THE TRAP

As we close out this book, we have one request: Don't fall into the trap.

What's the trap? It's reading everything we've included here and thinking that you're never the one that needs to improve. It's using this book as ammunition against others instead of as a mirror for yourself.

---

83 That said, if you unveil this idea to your superiors and they are actively against it, we suggest working to educate them more before "going rogue." That doesn't benefit you in the long run. We would also suggest changing the ask: request their sign-off on the simple step of implementing 1-on-1 meetings with your subordinates. Sometimes a smaller, more digestible, ask can produce results.

Former Navy SEAL Jocko Willink's bestselling book *Extreme Ownership* sums it up best: "Leaders must own everything in their world. There is no one else to blame."[84]

In fact, a few years after publishing the book, I heard Willink say the most common request he gets from leaders is to come and teach their team how to take more ownership. His response? "You've missed the point of the book." Why? Because the way to get others to take ownership is for you to take ownership first. That's it. That's how you do it. It isn't about a seminar, or a talk, or some sort of five-step plan. It all starts with you, the leader.

It's true that you have likely encountered thoughts and ideas that will be good for others to hear. But change has to start with you. Leadership starts with you. Ownership starts with you. That's why we included the practical next steps above. Don't be so preoccupied with what others need to hear that you miss the obvious steps you can take now.

Remember the Bob story from the Introduction and the Nigel story from Chapter 1? It's likely that many of you read those stories and thought, "I know one of those people!"

But what if you're the Bob? What if you're the Nigel? No one wants to think that could be the case, but if we're being honest, there are times in our lives when we've been either Bob or Nigel – or both.

In order to become a good leader, you have to realize that you're only one day – sometimes even one bad decision – away from being a Bob or a Nigel. Why? Because people management is the easy way. It's the quick way. It's the comfortable way. People development, in contrast, requires more work. It requires dedication. It requires intentionality.

---

84 Jocko Willink and Leif Babin, Extreme Ownership: How U.S. Navy SEALS Lead and Win (New York: St. Martin's Press, 2017, Kindle Edition), 13.

The truth is, we all have a Bob or a Nigel inside of us, and we have to work every day to make sure he never wins out. For many people, Bob or Nigel doesn't come out intentionally – Bob or Nigel comes out because we get lazy, we get complacent, or we get tired.

No one wakes up in the morning truly wanting to be a Nigel or a Bob. The goal is to make sure you don't go to bed that way.

So how do you combat that? An important way is to ask for feedback. As leaders, we regularly send out anonymous surveys asking for people to rate our performance as well as answer open-ended questions. Questions like, "What is it like to work with me?"

Many of us might expect to get all sorts of flowery things back. And while we receive that, there are also plenty of times when we get feedback that we didn't expect. When you get that tough feedback, you have two options: You can deflect and cast blame, or you can take a look in the mirror.

We implore you to look in the mirror.

When you look in the mirror, you have to ask yourself the hard questions:

- What am I doing that contributes to these feelings?
- What can I do better?
- Where is the communication breaking down?
- What do I need to change?

In other words, don't just receive the feedback but listen to the feedback. And then use it to grow. Don't put blinders on. Why? Because blinders create, well, blind spots. And blind spots are both leadership-killers and business-killers.

We'll end with this: No one is as good of a leader as they think they are. We're not. We have blind spots that we need others to call out. We have our Bob and Nigel moments. But here's what we've learned: People development doesn't require perfection; it requires humility. It requires you to constantly evaluate yourself, constantly grow, and constantly strive for the best version of yourself. That's not easy. But it is necessary.

So here's where we throw you a bit of a curveball. We discussed in the introduction how the last five chapters form the foundation of people management. That's still true, but there's a caveat: There's something deeper than a foundation. A foundation is good. But what's even more sturdy, what's even more unchanging, lies far below the surface. It's bedrock.

Humility is the bedrock of people development. It makes all of this possible. It supports everything else. Without bedrock, you can't even build a foundation. Without humility, you have nothing. None of this works without humility.

And if there's one thing we've learned, it's that leadership will humble you. It's humbled us. But can we tell you something? It's worth it. It's so worth it. Because humility makes people development possible, and people development – because it's the future – will free you up, unlock employee retention, and skyrocket your organization's growth.

So, with that said, we'll end this book with how we began it. People development is the new way forward. It's not a fad; it's a foundation. Ignore it, and you'll be left behind. Embrace it, and you'll be a part of the revolution. Implement it, and you'll reap the incredible benefits.

So welcome to the revolution.

ACKNOWLEDGMENTS

CHRIS

Creating a book like this takes more work than even we understood when we set out to write it. And while our names are on the front cover, the actual content would not have been possible without some key people that we need to recognize.

First, I would like to acknowledge my wife, Sarah, and our three kids. They have moved across the world, endured countless long nights, early mornings, and changes of plans over the years. Thank you for your support and dedication.

Second, it's critical to call out the numerous amazing teams we have had the opportunity to serve with both at Pushpay and at Leadr. You have made us – and me – what we are today. Every single one of you has helped us learn and grow. Thank you!

I also want to thank the writers, editors, and leaders who helped during this process – the ones who helped us find our voice, edit it, and turn this into something we are deeply proud of, specifically Jonathon M. Seidl, Kristen Orlowski, Anna Baker, and Holly Tate. Thank you for your patience and your expertise.

Finally, I can't stress enough the benefit of avid reading to further your own growth and development. We would not be here today without the thoughtful words and insights of people like Jim Collins, Seth Godin, John Maxwell, Jocko Willink, Patrick Lencioni, and numerous others. Their words have been critical, and we encourage you to soak them up as well.

MATT

They say it takes a village to raise a child. If that's true, I think it takes a city to help us continue developing as adults. That city has definitely surrounded us.

That's because this book is the culmination of so many people, events, ideas, and, ultimately, stories. None of it would have been possible if it weren't for all of those who committed to the journey with us along the way. Thank you for bearing with us and offering your hearts, minds, and dedication.

There's that old saying that any success you experience today is because you're "standing on the shoulders of giants." For those giants out there who were the foundation for my growth – and you know who you are – thank you. More specifically, I'd like to thank Ross Shannon, Bradden du Jary, Scott Thornton, Joe Sweeney, Jeremy Bohnett, Peter Wooster, and Holly Tate. Each one of you has affected me in a unique and special way.

I'd also like to acknowledge Jonathon M. Seidl of The Veritas Creative for helping us see the vision for this book and helping it become a reality, as well as the tireless efforts and long hours of Kristen Orlowski, Anna Baker, and (once again) Holly Tate.

On a more personal note, I'd like to thank my wife, Kiasa. I said it at the beginning, but I need to say it again: None of this would be possible without your love and support over the years. You are a beautiful person inside and out.

I can't leave without also thanking my dad, who inspired me to be an avid reader at a young age. I read *The Hobbit* cover-to-cover when I was eight, and I've never looked back. I'm still averaging 60 books a year because of the love for reading you instilled in me. To that end, I want to echo what Chris said above: You will never regret reading one more book, listening to one more podcast, or watching one more video. Always stay hungry to learn!

On that note, one final thought. The best way to grow is by doing. I grew the most when I traveled across the world for a 100% commission-based role with no guarantees of success. It challenged me. It grew me. It changed me. Never shy away from doing challenging things. More often, you'll regret what you don't do versus what you actually do.

APPENDIX A

CH. 3: UNIQUE STRENGTHS

Before you can coach someone to develop and utilize their strengths, you have to identify them. That's where personality assessments come in. Here are some of the most popular workplace assessments used to empower more valuable communication, development, and productivity.

Myers Briggs[85] - Katharine Cook Briggs and Isabel Briggs Myers, a mother-daughter team, were pioneers in developing this personality assessment, which is based on the psychological principles of Carl Jung. This type is expressed in 16 different combinations of four preferences, based on how each person uses perception and judgment in the world. Isabel once said, "when people differ, a knowledge of type lessens friction and eases strain. In addition, it reveals the value of differences. No one has to be good at everything."

Use Cases: Myers Briggs is a well-rounded assessment for a diverse team. It can help you determine which areas someone is strongest in, making it ideal for leadership development and relationship building. Recognizing that not every person has to be good at everything helps each individual dive into their strengths and feel comfortable developing their weaknesses. Myers Briggs is used by numerous companies around the globe, including consulting firms, McKinsey, Bain, Deloitte, and Accenture, to name a few.

---

85 The Myers & Briggs Foundation. https://www.myersbriggs.org/

DiSC[86] - The DiSC Assessment is a simpler assessment: After a test that gauges how you respond to challenges, how you influence others, your preferred pace, and how you respond to rules and procedures, you receive a scaled color-coded map showing where you fall in four categories of personality: dominance (D), influence (i), steadiness (S), and conscientiousness (C). This test measures tendencies and preferences, or patterns of behavior, and is a great way to start a conversation - or know how to communicate well with others on your team as you learn which "color" is highest for them.

Use Cases: DiSC is easy to implement in the workplace because of its simplicity. Your staff only needs to understand 4 "types" and which of their colleagues is high or low in those areas. While simplicity can be beneficial, also remember that our personalities are complex. Trying to minimize people into one of four types can leave room for confusion or misunderstanding. Organizations such as American Express, AT&T, Blue Cross/Blue Shield, and Boeing use DiSC to build stronger teams in the workplace.

Enneagram[87] - The Enneagram may arguably be the most fun and interpersonal assessment, but it can also be a great tool to use in a work context. A simple evaluation reveals where participants fall into nine different types, with a range of more complex discussion points, including wings, dominant types, and more.

Use Cases: By understanding how you connect, react to, and perceive the world, you can then dive deeper into how each type interacts with others and perceives itself as driven by core tendencies, or "centers," and what growth or stress trajectories look like for each type. This is a perfect starting place for leadership development as someone begins the journey toward leadership growth opportunities. Once you know what your 'self' looks like in growth, it's much easier to visualize and tackle a plan for how to get there. Organizations including Toyota, Avon, and The CIA use the enneagram for leadership development.

---

86 Disc Profile. https://www.discprofile.com/

87 The Enneagram Institute. https://www.enneagraminstitute.com/

Strengths Finder[88] - Also known as CliftonStrengths, this assessment is best summed up through a quote from innovator Don Clifton who asked, "what would happen if we studied what was right with people versus what's wrong with people?" CliftonStrengths does just that: A thorough and thoughtful questionnaire leads test-takers to a series of 34 themes organized into four strengths categories.

Use Cases: This assessment will help your team clarify both what they uniquely do well and what they need help accomplishing from others. In other words, it highlights a list of strengths so your team can be empowered to lead from there with confidence.

Working Genius[89] - This is an assessment that Patrick Lencioni and The Table Group developed. It focuses on six areas of "genius" which you can remember by the acronym "Widget."

Use Cases: Lencioni says that he developed this model to help others discover their list of personal strengths or their "work genius" which ultimately leads them to both personal and professional joy and fulfillment. For leaders, this means higher engagement and higher productivity.

Regardless of which assessment you take, each of these tests is designed to help you tap into your personal strengths and coach others to do the same. You may find that it encourages you in your role, or motivates you to pursue an opportunity that is truly a passion and a calling.

---

88 CliftonStrengths, Gallup https://www.gallup.com/cliftonstrengths/en/strengthsfinder.aspx

89 The Table Group, "The Six Types of Working Genius." Working Genius. https://www.workinggenius.com/

APPENDIX B

Personalized Plan for Employee Name

Content/ Project	Due Month 1	Due Month 2	Due Month 3	Due Month 4	Due Month 5
Books	The 5 Dysfunctions of a Team	Radical Candor	The Go Giver & The Go Giver Leadr	Manager chooses book & creates the assignment	Student chooses book & writes a one page report
Learning Assignments	#1: Steve Jobs' 2005 Stanford Commencement Address #2: One-on-ones are my most valuable meetings; here's how I run them	#3: Start with Why: Simon Sinek #4: How to Find Meaningful Work: EntreLeadership	#5: The Heart of Daring Leadership- Brené Brown #6: John C. Maxwell "The Rule of 5 for Lifting Your Lid	Manager chooses 2 Podcast / Video/ Blog & Creates assignment	Student chooses 1 Podcast/ Video / Blog & writes a 250 word summary
Executive Coffees	SVP of Growth	Executive Chairman & Co-Founder	CEO & Co-Founder	VP Product & Engineering	CFO
Peer-to-Peer Coaching	Session on ____	Session on ____	Session on ____	Session on ____	Session on ____
Stretch Projects	⟶	⟶	⟶	⟶	⟶

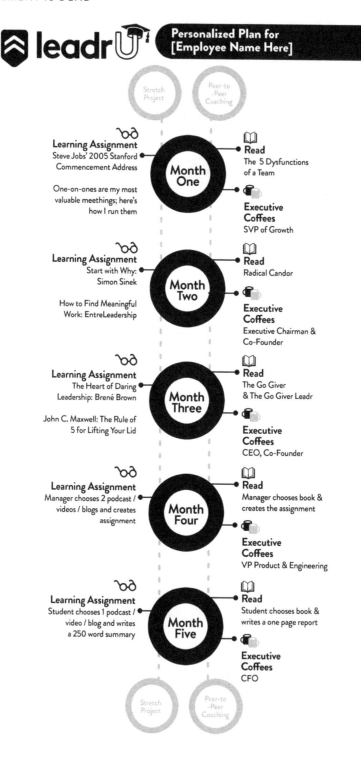

leadr U
**Personalized Plan for
[Employee Name Here]**

Stretch Project

Peer-to-Peer Coaching

Learning Assignment
Steve Jobs' 2005 Stanford
Commencement Address

One-on-ones are my most
valuable meethings; here's
how I run them

Month One

Read
The 5 Dysfunctions
of a Team

Executive Coffees
SVP of Growth

Learning Assignment
Start with Why:
Simon Sinek

How to Find Meaningful
Work: EntreLeadership

Month Two

Read
Radical Candor

Executive Coffees
Executive Chairman &
Co-Founder

Learning Assignment
The Heart of Daring
Leadership: Brené Brown

John C. Maxwell: The Rule of
5 for Lifting Your Lid

Month Three

Read
The Go Giver
& The Go Giver Leadr

Executive Coffees
CEO, Co-Founder

Learning Assignment
Manager chooses 2 podcast /
videos / blogs and creates
assignment

Month Four

Read
Manager chooses book &
creates the assignment

Executive Coffees
VP Product & Engineering

Learning Assignment
Student chooses 1 podcast /
video / blog and writes
a 250 word summary

Month Five

Read
Student chooses book &
writes a one page report

Executive Coffees
CFO

Stretch Project

Peer-to-Peer Coaching

To save you time communicating all of this to your team, here's a sample email you can send out outlining all of the details. We also recommend having an optional informational meeting a week or two before your development program kickoff to address any questions.

You can also find these templates at leadr.com/growth-plan.

Hey Team,

So Listen:

94% of employees say they would stay at a company longer if it invested in their career development. That's a big percentage, and it's not to be ignored!

Here at _____, we are committed to investing in each and every one of our staff [that's YOU!], in leadership and career development. One of our ways to invest in you is through our leadership development program, and we are ready for our next class to begin!

Orientation is on _____, and if you've been here for around 90 days, we would love for you to participate. We may even sneak you in if you are on the 75-80 day mark :)

See info below...

What does LeadrU look like?

5 Month Program
- 5 Books Read
- 5 Hours spent with the Exec Team 10 Learning Assignments
- 1 Stretch Project

- Group Discussions
- New Leadership Opportunities

What Are My Next Steps?

1. Reply to me and let me know you want to join the leadership development program for this session.

2. Set up a meeting, this week or next, with your manager and do the following to fill out your LeadrU Personalized Plan: Make a copy of this sheet (link to the first chart found in this section) and you and your manager should fill out the highlighted sections.

3. Send me the following by _____:

- Completed LeadrU personalized Plan
- The list of books that are on your plan that you will need.

We will purchase these for you as a thank you for investing in your professional development!

We can't wait to learn together!

APPENDIX C

CH. 5: GOALS

USEFUL GOAL TEMPLATES
TO TRACK AND REPORT

The secret sauce to success in goal setting is to identify a method for planning and tracking that works for you. The good news is that you do not have to start from scratch in designing a system. There are dozens of tools and templates available that run the gamut, from simple spreadsheets to sophisticated people management software.

Goal templates help us refine our ideas and desires. They also create order in the chaos, allowing everyone in the organization to follow the same model. Effective templates are versatile enough to work for everyone, from the executive suite to the frontline desk. They can be used for personal and professional aspirations, and they can be recycled from year to year or goal to goal.

If you are just getting started with goal setting or have limited resources, Office 365 offers several useful templates:

- The SMART Goals template in PowerPoint is a great starter tool for introducing the concept at a staff meeting or sharing it with a remote workforce. The prompts and examples guide planners through the process of identifying and finalizing goals. Employees will also benefit from reviewing this insightful list of SMART goal examples for businesses[90] from inbound marketing specialist Bluleadz.

- If you are new to goal setting and not ready to invest in a software program, then you can download an efficient Idea Planner template in Excel. Transfer each goal and objective into the spreadsheet, and then identify action steps and resources needed. There are also fields for assigning tasks and due dates as well as tracking the project status.

If you'd like to give the goal-setting framework known as Objectives and Key Results (OKRs) a try, this starter kit[91] goes through the process step by step, including free access to a simple worksheet.

For those looking to roll out a comprehensive goal program across an entire organization, goal-setting software will be the best choice. At Leadr, we've built the next generation of people management software to unify disconnected efforts and measure real-time progress.

Our software provides visibility into company, team, and individual goals over time, allowing managers to continually assess efforts and deliver feedback from a coaching standpoint. Leadr is designed to support a variety of goal frameworks, including OKRs, and will serve as the central place for all your company's growth and development activities.

---

90 Baylor Cherry, "28 SMART Goal Examples (+Template) That Will Help You Succeed." BluLeadz, May 2019. https://www.bluleadz.com/blog/top-3-smart-goal-examples

91 John Doerr, "Measure What Matters OKR Starter Kit." Coda. https://coda.io/@johndoerr/measure-what-matters-starter-kit-by-john-doerr